CREATING CHARACTER ARCS

The Masterful Author's Guide to
Uniting Story Structure, Plot,
and Character Development

CREATING
CHARACTER
ARCS

The Masterful Author's Guide to
Uniting Story Structure, Plot,
and Character Development

K.M. WEILAND

The Masterful Author's Guide to Uniting Story Structure, Plot, and Character Development

Published by PenForASword Publishing

ISBN-13: 978-1-944936-04-4

Dedicated to my beloved Savior,
who shows me His Truths, helps me overcome my Lies,
and leads me to positive change every single day.
(Deut. 30:19-20a)

To Lorna, who is a listening ear and a mouth of encouragement,
as both a friend and a fellow writer.

Also by K.M. Weiland:

Behold the Dawn

Dreamlander

Storming

Wayfarer

Non-Fiction

Outlining Your Novel

Outlining Your Novel Workbook

Structuring Your Novel

Structuring Your Novel Workbook

Creating Character Arcs Workbook

Writing Your Story's Theme

Writing Archetypal Character Arcs

Jane Eyre: The Writer's Digest Annotated Classic

Conquering Writer's Block and Summoning Inspiration

5 Secrets of Story Structure

TABLE OF CONTENTS

What Is the Lie?
Symptoms of the Lie
Further Examples of the Lie the Character Believes
Questions to Ask About the Lie Your Character
Believes

What Your Character Wants
What Your Character Needs
Further Examples of the Thing the Character Wants
and the Thing the Character Needs
Questions to Ask About the Thing the Character
Wants and the Thing the Character Needs

What Is Your Character's Ghost?
Further Examples of Your Character's Ghost
Questions to Ask About Your Character's Ghost

Your Protagonist's Characteristic Moment
Convince Readers to Invest in Your Character
Create a Memorable Scene
What Is a Characteristic Moment?
Further Examples of the Characteristic Moment
Questions to Ask About Your Characteristic Moment

Possible Manifestations of the Normal World
The Symbolism of the Normal World
How to Create Your Story's Normal World
What Is the Normal World

Further Examples of the Character's Arc in the Third Act
Questions to Ask About Your Character's Arc in the Third Act

Timing the Final Rejection of the Lie Your Character Believes
The Climactic Moment
How Does the Climax Manifest in Character Arcs?
Further Examples of the Climax in Character Arcs
Questions to Ask About Your Character's Arc in the Climax

The Thematic Question
The Character's New Normal
How Does the Resolution Manifest in Character Arcs?
Further Examples of the Resolution in Character Arcs
Questions to Ask About Your Character's Arc in the
  Resolution.

The Truth the Character Believes
The Normal World
The Characteristic Moment
The First Act
How Does the First Act Manifest in a Flat Arc?
Questions to Ask About the First Act in a Flat Arc

The First Plot Point
The First Half of the Second Act
The Midpoint
The Second Half of the Second Act
How Does the Second Act Manifest in a Flat Arc?
Questions to Ask About the Second Act in a Flat Arc

The Third Plot Point
The Third Act
The Climax

Where Does Your Character's Arc End?
Double Check Your Character's Arc

Introduction

CAN YOU STRUCTURE CHARACTERS?

W HAT IF THERE were a sure-fire secret to creating stunning character arcs? Would you be interested in discovering it? If you care about connecting with readers, grabbing their emotions, and creating stories that will resonate on a level deeper than mere entertainment, then the answer has to be a resounding *yes!*

But here's the thing about character arcs: they're way too easy to take for granted. On the surface, character arcs seem to boil down to nothing more than a simple three-step process:

1. The protagonist starts one way.

2. The protagonist learns some lessons throughout the story.

3. The protagonist ends in a (probably) better place.

That's character arc in a nutshell. Easy-peasy, lemon squeezy. What's to learn? Turns out: *a lot.*

THE LINK BETWEEN CHARACTER ARCS AND STORY STRUCTURE

Too often, character and plot are viewed as separate entities—to the point that we often pit them against each other, trying to determine which is more important. But nothing could be further from the truth. Plot and character are integral to one another. Remove either one from the equation (or even just try to approach them as if they were independent of one another), and you risk creating a story that may have awesome *parts*, but which will not be an awesome *whole*.

We often think of plot as being about structure, but our notions of character and character arc tend toward the more airy-fairy. Surely, character arc is something that must evolve organically from the characters themselves. Surely, we can't *structure* our character arcs without making them formulaic or robbing them of life and spontaneity.

Surely, right?

Wrong, actually. When we say plot and character are integral to one another, what we're really saying is that plot *structure* and character *arc* are integral to one another. In his classic guide *Story*, Robert McKee says:

> We cannot ask which is more important, structure or character, because structure is character; character is structure. They're the same thing, and therefore one cannot be more important than the other.

If you're familiar with the basics of story structure (such as I talk about in my book *Structuring Your Novel*), then you can probably already see some of this structuring of character arc in action. The Major Plot Points all revolve around the character's actions and reactions. As Michael Hauge says in *Writing Screenplays That Sell*:

> The three acts of the [story] correspond to the three stages of the hero's outer motivation. Each change in the hero's motivation signals the arrival of the next act.

The character drives the plot, and the plot molds the character's arc. They cannot work independently.

THE LINK BETWEEN CHARACTER AND THEME

But it gets better! Not only does character arc directly influence story structure, it is also a direct influence on theme. In some respects, we might even go so far as to say that *character arc = theme.*

On even the surface level, the discovery of the integrality of these three most important of all story elements is thrilling. None of them lives in a vacuum. They are all symbiotic.

This makes the creation of all three both a little more complicated and, at the same time, a whole lot easier. It's more complicated for the obvious reason that we have three times as many story elements to keep track of at once. But it simplifies the overall process by rolling all three into a cohesive whole. Once you understand how plot, character, and theme all work together, chances are good that, if you get one of them right, you'll get all three right.

THE THREE BASIC CHARACTER ARCS

Although the possibilities for character development are as endless as the vagaries of human nature, we can narrow character arcs down to three basic types, with a few primary variations upon each:

The Positive Change Arc

This is the most popular and often the most resonant character arc. The protagonist will start out with varying levels of personal unfulfillment and denial. Over the course of the story, he will be forced to challenge his beliefs about himself and the world, until finally he conquers his inner demons (and, as a result, probably his outer antagonists as well) and ends his arc having changed in a positive way.

The Flat Arc

Many popular stories feature characters who are already essentially complete unto themselves. They're already heroes and don't require any noticeable personal growth to gain the inner strength to defeat the external antagonists. These characters experience little to no change over the course of the story, making their arcs static or "flat." These characters are the *catalysts* for change in the story world around them, sparking prominent growth arcs in the minor characters.

The Negative Change Arc

Negative Change Arcs offer, arguably, more variations than either of the other arcs. However, at their most basic level, the Negative Change Arc is just a Positive Change Arc flipped on its head. Instead of a character who grows out of his faults into a better person, the Negative Change Arc presents a character who ends in a worse state than that in which he began the story.

Because the Positive Change Arc is both the most complicated of the three arcs and the most integral to understanding the other two arcs, we'll be spending the largest section of the book discussing the intricacies of how to evolve your character in a positive way.

How should you create your characters' arcs? Where do you find their foundation? How do the important moments in story structure affect (and are affected by) the important moments in character arc? In short, how does character arc *work*? And how can you crack the code and create a stunning character arc in every single story? Read on to find out!

PART 1:
THE POSITIVE
CHANGE ARC

"There is always room for at least two truths."
—Colum McCann

1

THE LIE THE CHARACTER BELIEVES

PEOPLE HATE CHANGE. We may sit around and wish our lives were different, but when the rubber really starts streaking the tarmac, we usually find ourselves wishing we could just hang out here in our safe and familiar haunts.

Characters are no different. They resist change just as staunchly as any of us—which is a good thing. Out of resistance comes conflict; out of conflict comes plot. This is just the first of many ways in which plot and character arcs are inextricable from one another. Whether the connection is immediately evident or not, the external plot is all about the character's inner journey.

Plot, in its simplest manifestation, is all about the protagonist's thwarted goal. He wants something, and he can't have it, so he keeps right on trying.

The Positive Change Arc, in its simplest manifestation, is all about the protagonist's changing priorities. He realizes the reason he's not getting what he wants in the plot is because either:

a) He wants the wrong thing.

b) His moral methods for achieving what he wants are all wrong.

In *Dramatica*, Melanie Anne Phillips and Chris Huntley point out:

> One of the most common mistakes made by authors of every level of experience is to create a problem for their Main Character that has nothing to do with the story at large. The reasoning behind this is not to separate the two, but usually occurs because an author works out a story and then realizes that he has not made it personal enough.

THE LIE THE CHARACTER BELIEVES

The Change Arc is all about the Lie Your Character Believes. His life may be horrible, or his life may seem pretty great. But festering under the surface, is the Lie.

In order for your character to evolve in a positive way, he has to start out with something lacking in his life, some reason that makes the change necessary. He is incomplete in some way, but not because he is lacking something external. A person in a prison camp can still be entirely whole and balanced on the inside, while someone floating in a Malibu mansion's swimming pool might be one miserable son of a gun.

Your character is incomplete on the *inside*. He is harboring some deeply held misconception about either himself, the world, or probably both. As you'll see in the next chapter, this misconception is going to prove a direct obstacle to his ability to fulfill his plot goal. In some instances, it may start out seeming to be a strength, but as the story progresses, it will become his Achilles heel.

Your character may not even realize he *has* a problem. In the First Act, his understanding of his deficiencies will be vague at best. He may not feel handicapped or even in denial about the Lie until the Inciting Event (at the 12% mark) and/or the First Plot Point (at the 25% mark) rock his world and begin peeling away his defenses. The First Act gives writers the time and space to introduce the Lie and demonstrate the character's entrenchment in it via his Normal World (which we'll also address more in Chapter 5).

WHAT IS THE LIE?

Your character's Lie could take any number of forms. For example, maybe he believes:

Thor: Might makes right.

Jane Eyre: The only way to earn love is through servitude.

Jurassic Park: Kids aren't worth taking care of.

Secondhand Lions: The people you love will always lie to you.

Toy Story: Your only worth is in being the favorite.

Three Kings: Money is to be treasured more than people.

Green Street Hooligans: The weak must always submit to the strong.

What About Bob?: People will only pay attention to you if they think you're crazy.

The Lie is a specific belief, which you should be able to state in one short sentence. It may include some qualifiers, as does Jane Eyre's. Her basic Lie is that *she isn't worthy to be loved,* but it's qualified by her additional belief that *she can earn love if she is willing to enslave herself to others, physically and emotionally.*

SYMPTOMS OF THE LIE

How do you find the Lie? First, examine your plot to see if the Lie might already be evident in the conflict. (We'll get into that more in the next chapter when we discuss the conflict between the Thing the Character Wants and the Thing the Character Needs.) Second, look at the character's actions—and especially his reactions. See if you can spot any of the following:

- Fear
- Extreme hurt
- Inability to forgive
- Guilt
- Horrible secrets
- Shame over something done or suffered

None of these *are* the Lie, but they're often products of the Lie. Your protagonist may be aware of the *symptoms* of the Lie in his life, even if he isn't yet able to recognize the Lie itself. More than that, he may want nothing more than to shed the negative symptom, but he *can't* because he can't get past his fundamental belief in the Lie.

For example, in my medieval novel *Behold the Dawn*, the protagonist Marcus Annan's Lie is that *some sins are too great to be forgiven*. His symptoms are *guilt, shame, secrets*, and *a destructive lifestyle*. He wants to be forgiven and to find happiness and fulfillment, but he just can't get past the Lie.

Angela Ackerman and Becca Puglisi do a great job of offering possible Lie symptoms (as well as some great character arc discussions) in their *Negative Trait Thesaurus*. If you find you're having trouble coming up with some good symptoms (or even a good Lie, for that matter), take a riffle through their book for some inspiration.

Further Examples of the Lie the Character Believes

A *Christmas Carol* by Charles Dickens: Ebenezer Scrooge's infamous holiday transformation is rooted in his mistaken belief that *a man's worth can only be measured by the amount of money he has earned*.

***Cars* directed by John Lasseter:** My favorite of all the Pixar movies is powered by selfish race car Lightning McQueen's ingrained belief in the Lie that *life is a one-man show*.

QUESTIONS TO ASK ABOUT THE LIE THE CHARACTER BELIEVES

1. What misconception does your protagonist have about himself or the world?

2. What is he lacking mentally, emotionally, or spiritually, as a result?

3. How is the interior Lie reflected in the character's exterior world?

4. When the story opens, is the Lie making his life miserable? If so, how?

5. If not, will the Inciting Event and/or the First Plot Point begin to make him uncomfortable as a result of his Lie?

6. Does your character's Lie require any qualifiers to narrow its focus?

7. What are the symptoms of your character's Lie?

The Lie Your Character Believes is the foundation for his character arc. This is what's wrong in his world. Once you know what's wrong, you then get to set about figuring out how to make it right.

"Two souls, alas, are housed within my breast,
And each will wrestle for the mastery there."
—Johann Wolfgang von Goethe

2

THE THINGS
YOUR CHARACTER
WANTS AND NEEDS

T HE LIE YOUR Character Believes is the reason for all character arcs. After all, if everything's hunky-dunky, why change? Think of the Lie as the cavity in a tooth. Everything might look shiny and white on the outside, but inside there's decay. If the character is ever to be happy, he's going to have to do some drilling to excavate the rot in his life.

But, like most of us with a rotten tooth, he's in denial. Even though he keeps biting on that tooth and pushing at it with his tongue, he doesn't want to admit he's got a problem. In order to avoid facing the painful reality of his Lie, he wants to pretend the problem is something else. Melanie Anne Phillips and Chris Huntley, once again:

> ...we know that characters often work not toward the real so-
> lution but to a perceived solution. And characters frequently
> grapple with a problem that is ultimately recognized as only a
> symptom of the real problem.

The Lie plays out in your character's life, and your story, through the conflict between the Thing He Needs (the Truth) and the Thing He Wants (the perceived cure for the *symptoms* of the Lie).

WHAT YOUR CHARACTER WANTS

The first intersection of character arc and plot is found in the protagonist's goal. What does he want? What's his major story goal? World domination? A wife? To survive? To die? To get a raise?

Every story starts with the character's goal. Simple enough, right? But that's just the plot. What about character?

That, my friends, is where this gets interesting. It isn't enough for us to create a story goal that's just a *surface* goal. To intertwine with the character arc, this goal needs to be an extension or reflection of something that matters to the character on a deeper level. He can't just want world domination and/or a wife because, hey, who doesn't? He has to want it for a soul-deep reason, one even he may not fully comprehend.

If you guessed that the Lie is at the root of that soul-deep reason, then you guessed right.

If only on a subconscious level, the character realizes he has a problem in his life. His problems may be evident in his miserable standard of living (Charles Dickens's *Little Dorrit*), or his problem may be an inner discontentment that manifests even in the midst of a seemingly perfect external life (Jon Turtel- taub's *The Kid*). But what he doesn't realize, subconsciously or otherwise, is the true solution—the Thing He Needs. Nope, he thinks that if he can just have what he Wants, all will be well.

What Is the Thing Your Character Wants?

The Thing Your Character Wants will almost always be something external, something physical. He's trying to salve his inner emptiness with exterior solutions. His problem is depression, but he's busily putting a cast on his arm. He thinks if he can just have that new job, that new trophy wife, that new set of golf clubs, everything will be perfect. He'll be rich, powerful, loved, respected—and fulfilled.

Here we are dissing The Thing Your Character Wants, but, really, it may be a perfectly worthy goal in its own right. He might want to:

Thor: Be king.

Jane Eyre: Be loved.

Jurassic Park: Study dinosaur bones in peace.

Secondhand Lions: Have a real home with his mother.

Toy Story: Be Andy's favorite toy.

Three Kings: Gain enough money to be independent and happy.

Green Street Hooligans: Graduate college.

What About Bob?: Be cured of mental problems.

Nothing wrong with any of those. But the problem for these characters is that they're pursuing goals that are furthering their enslavement to their Lies. They're not pursuing happiness and fulfillment holistically by addressing the Lie. Rather, they're trying to get what they want *in spite of* their refusal to buck up and look deep into the darkness of their own souls.

What Your Character Needs

In a word, the Thing Your Character Needs is the Truth. He needs the personalized antidote to his Lie. This is the most important thing in his life. If he misses out on this Truth, he is never going to be able to grow in a positive way. He's either going to remain stuck in his current internal predicament forever, or he's going to digress into an even worse state (as we'll see when we study the Negative Change Arc later on in Part 3).

Your character will spend most of the story pursuing an outer, plot-related goal related to the Thing He Wants. But what the story is really about, on a deeper level, is his growth into a place where he, first subconsciously, then consciously, recognizes and pursues his inner goal—the Thing He Needs.

What Is the Thing Your Character Needs?

The Thing Your Character Needs usually won't be something

physical—although it can (and usually should) take on a physical or visual manifestation by the end of the story. The Thing Your Character Needs is usually going to be nothing more than a realization. In some stories, this realization may change nothing about his external life, but it will always transform his perspective of himself and the world around him, leaving him more capable of coping with his remaining external problems.

The Thing Your Character Needs may preclude the Thing He Wants. He will invariably have to come to a point where he's willing to sacrifice What He Wants in order to secure What He Needs. Sometimes the story will have to end on that bittersweet note of interior gain and exterior loss. But, other times, once the character has embraced the Thing He Needs, he will then be all the more empowered in his pursuit of What He Wants—allowing him to harmonize both his inner and outer goals in the finale.

The Thing Your Character Needs might be to:

Thor: Learn humility and compassion.

Jane Eyre: Embrace spiritual freedom.

Jurassic Park: Protect the living future over the dead past.

Secondhand Lions: Have faith in people.

Toy Story: Be able to share Andy's love.

Three Kings: Find a cause worth fighting for.

Green Street Hooligans: Find the courage to stand up for himself.

What About Bob?: Be loved for who he is.

As you can see, these are all incorporeal concepts. But they are all things that can be demonstrated physically and visually because they demand the characters act upon their new beliefs, once they've claimed them.

FURTHER EXAMPLES OF THE THINGS THE CHARACTER WANTS AND NEEDS

A Christmas Carol: The Thing Scrooge Wants is to make as much money as possible, no matter how many people he has to run over to get it. The Thing He Needs is to remember that true wealth is found in the love of his fellow human beings.

Cars: The Thing Lightning McQueen Wants is to become the world's most famous race car by winning the Piston Cup and gaining a Dinoco sponsorship. The Thing He Needs is to let others into his life by helping them and allowing them to help him.

QUESTIONS TO ASK ABOUT THE THINGS THE CHARACTER WANTS AND NEEDS

1. How is the Lie holding your character back?

2. How is the Lie making your character unhappy or unfulfilled?

3. What Truth does your character Need to disprove the Lie?

4. How will he learn this Truth?

5. What does your character Want more than anything?

6. How is his plot goal related to or an extension of the Thing He Wants?

7. Does he believe the Thing He Wants will solve his personal problems?

8. Is the Thing He Wants holding him back from the Thing He Needs?

9. Does the Thing He Needs preclude his gaining the Thing He Wants—or will he only be able to gain the Thing He Wants *after* he has found the Thing He Needs?

10. How will his life be different once he embraces the Thing He Needs?

Your protagonist's inner conflict is all about this silent war between his Want and his Need. But it's also the gasoline in the engine of the outer conflict. If you have these two elements working in concert, you'll also have plot and character well on their way to perfect harmony.

"History, despite its wrenching pain,
cannot be unlived,
but if faced with courage,
need not be lived again."
—Maya Angelou

3

YOUR CHARACTER'S GHOST

WHAT IS YOUR character's Ghost, and how does it affect his character arc? Once you've figured out the Lie Your Character Believes, as well as the Thing He Wants and the Thing He Needs, the next question is: *Why* does the character believe the Lie in the first place? To find the answer, start looking for something ghostly in your character's past!

If there's one solid rule in fiction, it's that every effect must have a cause. If your character is in need of undergoing a Change Arc, then one of your first tasks is figuring out *why* he needs to change. What happened to cause him to embrace this obviously damaging Lie?

Humans are survivors. We'll do anything we can to move toward life, comfort, and peace. But we're also self-destructive. We can focus so tightly on one aspect of survival that we sacrifice other elements. In our quest to be top dog in our chosen careers, we can sacrifice our emotional health through poor relationship choices and our physical health through poor lifestyle choices. Worse than that, we're usually deliberately blind to our destructive behaviors. We rationalize our actions and convince ourselves—rightly or wrongly—that the end justifies the means.

In other words, we *lie* to ourselves. But there's always a reason for that Lie. There's always a reason why we value survival in one aspect of our lives over survival in another. Sometimes these reasons are obvious (you have to earn enough money to eat, even if it means busting your back day in and day out). But other times, the reasons are so obscure even you don't recognize them (you have to work like a dog to earn a six-figure income or you'll feel like the loser your father always said you were).

Find the reason, and you'll find the Ghost.

YOUR CHARACTER'S GHOST

"Ghost" is movie speak for something in your character's past that haunts him. You may also see it sometimes referred to as the "wound." In their fabulous *Negative Trait Thesaurus*, Angela Ackerman and Becca Puglisi explain:

> Wounds are often kept secret from others because embedded within them is **the lie**—an untruth that the character believes about himself.… For example, if a man believes he is unworthy of love (*the lie*) because he was unable to stop his fiancée from being shot during a robbery (*the wound*), he may adopt attitudes, habits, and negative traits that make him undesirable to other women.

Often, the wound will be something shocking and traumatic (such as the massacre of the French and Indians at Ft. Charles that haunts Benjamin Martin in Roland Emmerich's *The Patriot* or Jason Bourne's forgotten past as an assassin in Robert Ludlum's *The Bourne Identity*). But it can also be something smaller and more ordinary, such as a breakup (Jane Austen's *Persuasion*), a stressful parental relationship (Barry Levinson's *Rain Man*), or physical inferiority (Mike Wazowski in Dan Scanlon's *Monsters University*).

The bigger and more destructive the Lie, the more shocking and impactful the Ghost should be. Or to flip that on its head: the bigger the Ghost, the bigger the Lie, the bigger the arc.

The Ghost will often be a part of your character's backstory, and readers will discover it only bit by bit. In these cases, the

Ghost can often provide a tantalizing mystery. The *why* behind your character's belief in the Lie will hook readers' curiosity, and you can string them along for most of the book with only little clues, until finally the Ghost is presented in a grand reveal toward the end.

In other stories, we may never discover the specifics about the Ghost. The character may have an obviously significant past, but it remains cloaked in secrecy. Or his past, in itself, may not seem so interesting, even though it obviously contributed in some way to his Lie, and the author chooses not to reveal it.

In still other stories, the Ghost's cause may be dramatized in the First Act, in a prologue of sorts. This is particularly prominent in origins stories, such as Sam Raimi's first *Spider-Man* movie and Christopher Nolan's *Batman Begins*. Here, the Ghost segment is a story unto itself that explains the protagonist's motivations, before the book or movie moves on to the real story. In these stories, the character probably won't start out believing in a Lie in Chapter One. Only once the Ghost has appeared and changed his Normal World will he find himself struggling to justify his new mindsets and actions. In *The Writer's Journey*, Christopher Vogler notes:

> Other stories show the hero as essentially complete until a close friend or relative is kidnapped or killed in the first act.

What Is Your Character's Ghost?

Your character's Ghost may take any number of forms. The Ghost may be:

Thor: The promise that Thor would grow up to be king, regardless his personal merits.

Jane Eyre: Jane's aunt's refusal to love her.

Jurassic Park: [Unstated.]

Secondhand Lions: Walter's mother's pathological deceit.

Toy Story: Knowledge of what happens to unloved toys.

Three Kings: Disillusionment about an Army career.

Green Street Hooligans: An absentee father.

What About Bob?: A divorce.

The Ghost may be as simple as an ingrained belief (Jane Eyre's aunt tells her she's wicked and worthless, and, deep down, Jane believes her). The Ghost may be something obviously horrific that the protagonist did (as in *The Patriot*) or that was done to him or someone he loved (as in *Spider-Man*), or the Ghost may be something the protagonist embraces without realizing the damage it's causing (as in *Thor*). The key to identifying the Ghost is understanding it will always be the underlying cause for the protagonist's belief in the Lie.

FURTHER EXAMPLES OF YOUR CHARACTER'S GHOST

A Christmas Carol: Scrooge has a superfluity of literal ghosts flying around his story, and one of them—the Ghost of Christmas Past—gives us a front-row seat to the figurative Ghost in Scrooge's backstory. Turns out he had a wretched childhood, thanks to a father who never showed him affection and locked him away at a boarding school, even during the Christmas holidays.

Cars: We're never told about Lightning McQueen's Ghost. The race commentators say, "The rookie sensation came into the season unknown"—and that is largely how he comes into the movie. We never discover why he's so intent on being free from depending on others.

QUESTIONS TO ASK ABOUT YOUR CHARACTER'S GHOST

1. Why does your character believe the Lie?

2. Is there a notable event in his past that has traumatized him?

3. If not, will there be a notable event in the First Act that will traumatize him?

4. Why does the character nourish the Lie?

5. How will he benefit from the Truth?

6. How "big" is your character's Ghost? If you made it bigger, would you end up with a stronger arc?

7. Where will you reveal your character's Ghost? All at once early on? Or piece by piece throughout the story, with a big reveal toward the end?

8. Does your story *need* the Ghost to be revealed? Would it work better if you never revealed it?

Backstory is always one of the most interesting aspects of a character. In constructing yours, pay special attention to the Ghost. If you know what initiated your character's belief in the Lie, you're halfway to helping him overcome it.

"You take people,
you put them on a journey,
you give them peril,
you find out who they really are."
—Joss Whedon

4

THE CHARACTERISTIC MOMENT

FIRST IMPRESSIONS **DO** count. And your protagonist's Characteristic Moment is his first chance to impress your readers. Now that you've got the basic theory of character arc out of the way and have figured out how to set up your protagonist's inner conflict, via the Lie He Believes, the Thing He Wants, the Thing He Needs, and the Ghost—you're ready to officially begin *writing* your character's story.

The structure of character arc begins with the Characteristic Moment. Throughout the rest of Part 1, we'll be aligning the major moments in the character arc with the major structural plot points. (If you're unfamiliar with the basics of story structure, see my book *Structuring Your Novel*, which will provide a helpful foundation for the rest of this book's discussion.) The Characteristic Moment (and the Normal World, which we'll discuss in the next chapter) aligns with the Hook. It shows up the moment your protagonist does—presumably in the first chapter.

In real life, people are cautioned against making snap decisions about others, based on first impressions. But, face it: we do. And we're even less likely to feel conscientious about our judgments when reading fiction. We've just opened a book. We've never read this author before. We have no idea whether it's going to live up to its awesome back-cover blurb and prove worthy of our time. Then here comes the protagonist, prancing onstage. What's he doing? What's his personality? Does he seem like someone we're going to end up liking? Does he seem interesting? If not, we're already halfway to closing the book.

In short, a failed Characteristic Moment can mean a failed story.

YOUR PROTAGONIST'S CHARACTERISTIC MOMENT

The Characteristic Moment must accomplish several tasks. It must:

1. Introduce your protagonist.

2. (Probably) reveal your protagonist's name.

3. Indicate your protagonist's gender, age, nationality, and possibly his occupation.

4. Indicate important physical characteristics.

5. Indicate his role in the story (i.e., that he *is* the protagonist).

6. Demonstrate the prevailing aspect of his personality.

7. Hook readers' sympathy and/or their interest.

8. Show the protagonist's scene goal.

9. Indicate the protagonist's story goal.

10. Demonstrate, or at least hint at, the protagonist's Lie.

11. Influence the plot, preferably directly, but at the very least in a way that foreshadows later events.

This is quite a hefty checklist for the first scene of your story (especially when you add in related structural requirements). No wonder beginnings are so tough! The Characteristic Moment is a work of art. Don't settle for opening with your character doing any ol' thing. Select an event that will:

1. Make the protagonist appealing to readers.

2. Introduce both his strengths and his weaknesses.

3. Build the plot.

Convince Readers to Invest in Your Character

Even distilled down to these three aspects, the Characteristic Moment is still tricky. We need to indicate the character's "lack"—the problems in his life caused by the Lie—as soon as possible. But we don't want to focus too heavily on the character's negative aspects right away. In *Writing Screenplays That Sell*, Michael Hauge reinforces:

> You must establish identification with your hero before revealing major flaws that could reduce sympathy.

If your character's arc is all about his growing into courage, honesty, and selflessness, then he's going to have to start out as less than brave, truthful, or generous. But if you tried to open most stories with a selfish, cowardly liar, most readers probably wouldn't be hooked. And yet, what other kind of Characteristic Moment suggests itself for such a character? You must indicate his problems in order to prove how he's changed by the end of the story, right?

Absolutely. But your *foremost* job is hooking readers. If you intend your character to be generally likable, despite his faults, start with that. What do you *like* about him? What scene can you craft to highlight that? He doesn't have to be nice in this scene; he just has to be interesting. Ron Clement and Jon Musker's *Treasure Planet* opens with its rebellious teenage protagonist demonstrating his skills and courage aboard his "solar surfer." *The Kid* opens with its protagonist acting like a complete jerk, but his snide comments are so nasty (and accurate) that viewers can't look away.

Create a Memorable Scene

Think big. If your character's chief virtue is his compassion, don't settle for having him pat a stray dog. Have him run into NYC traffic just to cross the street and see why a little girl is crying. If he's known for his bravado, don't have him strut down the street. Have him pick a fight with five toughs—and win (or nearly).

Although optimally, you'll be able to work your character's Lie right into the Characteristic Moment, sometimes doing so just won't be possible. You can only keep so many balls in the air while still maintaining logic within the plot, which means you may occasionally have to postpone the introduction of the Lie until you've crossed off a few of your beginning's other requirements. However, that said, you need to introduce the Lie as quickly as possible. The Lie frames your character arc—and thus your entire story. Readers need proof of your character's weakness in order to understand what he will have to overcome.

What Is a Characteristic Moment?

Your protagonist's Characteristic Moment could manifest as:

Thor: A vow, as a child, to be like his father and grow up to "fight them all," and then, as an adult, a cocky display on his way to being announced heir to the throne—which illustrates key personality traits, the effects of the Lie, and the Thing He Wants Most.

Jane Eyre: A lonely moment, banned from the family circle, spent reading, and then a refusal to submit to her cousin's unjust cruelty—which illustrates both the Ghost and key personality traits.

Jurassic Park: An on-the-job demonstration of Dr. Grant's cranky inability to live in the modern world and his dislike of kids—which illustrates key personality traits, the Lie, and the Thing He Wants Most.

Secondhand Lions: A distrust of his mother's promises and a fearful attitude toward everything (especially pigs)—which illustrates the Lie, the Thing He Wants Most, and the personal weakness he will have to overcome.

Toy Story: A montage showing Woody being lovingly played with by Andy, and then, once he's "awake," a calm and organized leadership of the other toys—which illustrates the Thing He Wants Most and key personality traits.

Three Kings: A cynical but obviously intelligent response to babysitting a reporter—which illustrates the Ghost and key personality traits.

Green Street Hooligans: A grudging retreat from false accusations—which illustrates the Lie and the Thing He Wants Most.

What About Bob?: A hilariously neurotic morning routine—which illustrates the Thing He Wants Most and key personality traits.

Note that some Characteristic Moments are double-sided. Thor's Characteristic Moment takes place in a two-part series of scenes, the first of which is part of a prologue and shows him as a child. Just as with *Treasure Planet*, which also starts with a childhood prologue, the character must then be reestablished in his "true normal" as an adult with a second Characteristic Moment.

In *Jane Eyre* and *Toy Story*, you can see how you can use not just a single Characteristic Moment, but several to prove different aspects of your character. Jane shows us two sides of her personality—first her lonely, but contented introversion, then her defiant and spirited refusal to be trampled upon. Because of the constraints of *Toy Story*'s logic, in which the toys must be passive and still when humans are present, Woody's love for Andy is primarily shown through Andy's love for *him*. This is the most important aspect of the story, but we're also then given a prime example of Woody's able leadership of the other toys, once he "wakes up" in Andy's absence.

FURTHER EXAMPLES OF THE CHARACTERISTIC MOMENT

A Christmas Carol: Scrooge is introduced in a lengthy "telling" segment (not recommended for modern books), in which the author flat-out tells readers certain important facts about Scrooge's miserliness and general lack of the milk of human kindness. By the time we reach Scrooge's first dramatized scene, we already have a pretty clear picture of his personality. That picture is further emphasized when we enter his frigid counting house (heated by a "very small fire" and his employee Bob Cratchit's single coal), where he proceeds to reject his nephew's kindhearted Christmas invitation by telling him precisely what he thinks of the holiday and its goodwill toward men. Readers immediately get a sense of Scrooge's crabby personality, his incisive wit, his Lie (which he basically spells out), and his desire to make as much money as possible.

Cars: Lightning McQueen's intro comes by way of his verbalized pre-race routine, in which he claims, "I am speed" and "I eat losers for breakfast." He then demonstrates his sizable skills, as well as his disdain for his pit crew, in the lengthy race segment that opens the movie. Viewers are given further info, via the commentators, who reinforce Lightning's Lie by revealing he's already fired three pit crew chiefs because "he says he likes working alone." In this extended opening, viewers learn all they need to know about Lightning: his good points (his racing skills), his Lie, and the Thing He Wants Most (the Piston Cup).

QUESTIONS TO ASK ABOUT YOUR CHARACTERISTIC MOMENT

1. What important personality trait, virtue, or skill best sums up your protagonist?

2. How can you dramatize this trait to its fullest extent?

3. How can you dramatize this trait in a way that also introduces the plot?

4. How can you demonstrate your protagonist's belief in his Lie?

5. Can you reveal or hint at his Ghost?

6. How can you use this scene to reveal the Thing He Wants Most?

7. Does your protagonist's pursuit of both the overall goal and the scene goal meet with an obvious obstacle (i.e., conflict)?

8. How can you share important details about your protagonist (name, age, physical appearance) quickly and unobtrusively?

Don't settle for anything less than spectacular for your Characteristic Moment. This is your opportunity to create a fun and effective scene that will introduce readers to your character in a way they'll never forget—and from which they won't be able to look away.

"Stories do not happen in ordinary worlds—
stories happen when choices and events
propel the main character into a world
far more exciting, different and challenging
than the ordinary day-to-day
experience..."
—Charles Deemer

5

THE NORMAL WORLD

WHO WANTS TO read about a boring old Normal World? The Lost World? Sure! The Exciting, Unusual, Exotic, and Absolutely Thrilling World? You betcha. But the Normal World? Isn't that a pretty lame way to begin a story?

Nope. Not if you want your character's Change Arc to make sense, it isn't.

In the last chapter, you learned about how the Characteristic Moment ties into your story's Hook by introducing the protagonist, the Lie He Believes, the Thing He Wants, and the Thing He Needs. But the Characteristic Moment is only half of a good character arc's opening. It gives us character, but it still needs context. The Normal World provides that context.

People are largely defined by the microcosms in which they live. We are inevitably shaped by our surroundings, either because of the ways we fit in or the ways we don't. Just as inevitably, we are defined by our surroundings because they reflect our choices and limitations. How we came to be someplace, why we choose to remain there, or why we are forced to remain even if we don't want to—all these factors reveal interesting facets of our personalities, values, strengths, and weaknesses.

In a story, the Normal World will play an important role in the first quarter of your story—the First Act. This entire segment can basically be summarized as "setup," and the Normal

World plays a vital role in grounding the story in a concrete setting. Even more important, the Normal World creates the standard against which all the personal and plot changes to come will be measured. Without this vivid opening example of what will change in your character's life, the rest of the arc will lack definition and potency.

THE NORMAL WORLD

At its most basic level, the Normal World is—as its name suggests—a setting. This is the place in which your story opens. It is a place in which your character has found contentment—or at least complacency.

Possible Manifestations of the Normal World

The Normal World may seem wonderful on the surface (as in Tim Burton's *Edward Scissorhands* or Kurt Wimmer's *Equilibrium*), only to have its perfect façade cracked wide open, along with the character's misconceptions about the world and himself.

Or the Normal World may be safe but boring, with the protagonist chafing ineffectually against it without making any real effort to move on with his life (as in George Lucas's *A New Hope* or Robert Schwentke's *RED*).

Or the Normal World may be pretty lousy, but the protagonist is at least temporarily stuck there against his will (as in John Sturges's *The Great Escape* or Steven Spielberg's *Saving Private Ryan*).

Or the Normal World may be legitimately great, but the protagonist isn't yet ready to appreciate it or is being temporarily held back by the Normal World's advantages (as in L. Frank Baum's *The Wizard of Oz* or Frank Capra's *It's a Wonderful Life*).

Or the Normal World may present one set of challenges, which the protagonist finds himself unequipped to deal with until after he's experienced life beyond the Normal World (as in Pete Docter and Bob Peterson's *Up* and Chris Buck and Jennifer Lee's *Frozen*).

The Symbolism of the Normal World

The point is that the Normal World is a place the protagonist either doesn't want to leave or can't leave. It's the staging ground for his grand adventure. Most of the time he will take the Normal World for granted and feel it's going to go on and on forever, but sometimes he'll start the story knowing the Normal World is just a temporary stopover (as in James Cameron's *Avatar*).

Think of the Normal World as a symbolic representation of your character's inner world. The Normal World dramatizes the Lie the Character Believes. It empowers the character in that Lie, giving him no reason to look beyond it. Only when the Normal World is challenged or abandoned at the First Plot Point is the protagonist's belief in that Lie shaken.

How to Create Your Story's Normal World

In creating your story's Normal World, first ask yourself what kind of world will provide the most logical backstory for why your character believes the Lie. Then consider how to enhance the Normal World by making it the comfiest place ever for that Lie to continue its existence. Note, however, this does not mean it necessarily has to be a comfy place for your protagonist. Sometimes he may seem outwardly comfy, while, deep down, the Lie is making him miserable.

Next, ask yourself how you can create a Normal World that will best contrast the "adventure world" to follow in the next two acts. Sometimes your protagonist will leave the Normal World behind entirely and enter a dramatically new and different setting (as in *Jane Eyre*, when Jane leaves Lowood School to be a governess at Thornfield Hall). Other times, your protagonist will remain in the original physical setting of the Normal World (as in Pete Docter's *Monsters, Inc.*), with only facets of the world changing (as when Boo's arrival throws Monstropolis into chaos). Either way, you want to strive for the most dramatic contrast possible between the worlds, in order to provide your character with as much incentive as possible to enact his change.

The Normal World is important because it visibly proves to readers (it *shows* them) your protagonist's "before" state. Either he's going to have to change enough to move out of this destructive place, or he's going to have to change enough to fit in and take advantage of this healthy place.

What Is the Normal World?

Your story's Normal World could be:

Thor: A peaceful and prosperous planet—which enables Thor's prideful misconceptions.

Jane Eyre: A stark and loveless childhood, first at Jane's aunt's, then at a boarding school for girls—which reinforces her belief in her unloveableness.

Jurassic Park: An archaeological dig in perpetual need of funding—which doesn't tie into Dr. Grant's Lie but does prompt his acceptance of an otherwise unacceptable proposal (visit Jurassic Park), which advances the plot.

Secondhand Lions: A rundown farm with two antisocial great-uncles—which at first reinforces Walter's general fear of everything.

Toy Story: Andy's room, where Woody is the boss—which reinforces his belief in the Lie.

Three Kings: The closing days of the Gulf War—which reinforces the devaluation of people and the disillusionment in industrialized war.

Green Street Hooligans: An American university—which reinforces Matt's Lie by allowing him to be unjustly accused and expelled.

What About Bob?: New York City—which reinforces Bob's general neuroticism and contrasts with the motif of "taking a vacation from your problems."

We have a great assortment of Normal Worlds here—everything from Thor's awesome but personally unchallenging world, to the horrible world in which Jane Eyre is trapped until she finally escapes, to *Secondhand Lions'* seemingly awful Normal World, which, by the First Plot Point, begins to morph into something pretty wonderful.

FURTHER EXAMPLES OF THE NORMAL WORLD

A Christmas Carol: Scrooge's Normal World is introduced via his frigid counting house, where he would rather suffer through the cold than spend a few extra shillings on a bigger fire. His cold, money-driven world is further illustrated through his perception of London and the revelation of his equally cold and loveless home. It's a visibly horrible world, in which Scrooge has convinced himself to be content in order to maintain his Lie and his pursuit of the Thing He Wants. The setting is a magnificently symbolic representation of Scrooge's inner world—dark, cold, and lonely. Dickens's time-travel element allows him to beautifully contrast the Normal World of the present with possibilities both bright and horrific.

Cars: At first glance, Lightning McQueen's world seems pretty great—all glitter and glamour. He's racing in the Piston Cup, the most important car race in the world, and the racetrack is a delightful place of euphoric fans, raw adrenaline, and shining prospects. It will stand in stark contrast to the slow and rusty world of Radiator Springs. For the moment, however, it seems to represent everything Lightning wants, even as it feeds his Lie and traps him in a downward spiral of selfishness and isolation.

QUESTIONS TO ASK ABOUT THE NORMAL WORLD

1. What setting will open your story?

2. How will this setting change at the First Plot Point?

3. How can you contrast the Normal World with the "adventure world" to follow?

4. How does the Normal World dramatize or symbolize your character's enslavement to the Lie?

5. How is the Normal World causing or empowering the Lie?

6. Why is your character in the Normal World?

7. If your character doesn't want to leave the Normal World, what is helping him mask the discomfort caused by his Lie?

8. If your character wants to leave, what's stopping him?

9. Will the character return to the Normal World at the end of the story?

10. If the Normal World is a legitimately good place, how will the protagonist need to change in order to appreciate it?

The Normal World presents the valuable opportunity to visually dramatize your character's Lie. Take full advantage of your story's Normal World and create an opening segment that will explode into readers' minds and perfectly set up the adventure to follow.

"An adventure is only an inconvenience rightly considered. An inconvenience is only an adventure wrongly considered."
—G.K. Chesterton

6

THE FIRST ACT

T HE FIRST ACT is one of my favorite parts of any story. Why? On the surface, the First Act seems to be the slowest part of the story—and it often is. It's just setup, after all, right?

True enough, except for that one little word *just*.

It isn't "just" setup; it's SETUP! It sets up the plot, but even more importantly, it sets up the character arcs.

As you've already seen in the previous chapters, the setup necessary to prepare for your First Act is pretty intensive. But once you've got the prep work of deciding upon the Lie Your Character Believes, the Thing He Wants, the Thing He Needs, his Ghost, his Characteristic Moment, and his Normal World (phew!) out of the way, the First Act itself is comparatively simple to piece together.

In *A Writer's Journey*, Christopher Vogler points out:

> [Stories] are often built in three acts, which can be regarded as representing 1) the hero's decision to act, 2) the action itself, and 3) the consequences of the action.

6 PARTS OF CHARACTER ARC IN THE FIRST ACT

Following are the six major elements of the Positive Change Arc that must be included in the First Act. Most of these elements can happen just about anywhere within that first quarter of your book. Use your understanding of your story and its necessary pacing to find the appropriate timing for these key moments in your character's arc.

1. Reinforce the Lie

The reinforcement of your character's Lie will begin in the first chapter, specifically through the revelation of the Thing He Wants and the Thing He Needs. His Characteristic Moment and his Normal World will both illustrate the Lie. Readers need to see how the character's internal problems are, in turn, causing external problems.

This reinforcement should continue throughout the First Act. Your character's Lie may have several facets, so feel free to take your time introducing each of them. You don't have to cram *everything* into the first chapter. Hook readers with a glimpse of the character's problems, then use the rest of the First Act to fill in the gaps.

> **For Example:** Thor's Lie is practically handed to him by his father who tells him straight out he was born to be king.

2. Indicate the Character's Potential to Overcome the Lie

Right from the beginning, readers need to glimpse at least a teeny promise that your character possesses the *capability* to change.

What specific quality will be intrinsic to your character's ability to fight his way out of the Lie? (Refer to Angela Ackerman and Becca Puglisi's *Positive Trait Thesaurus* for inspiration.) Even if your character hasn't yet fully developed this trait, hint right from the beginning that the seed is there.

> **For Example:** In *Toy Story*, Woody's ability to be a good friend is on display right from the start in his caring attitude toward the other toys in Andy's room— even if he's not yet ready to be a good friend to Buzz.

3. Provide the Character's First Step in Discovering How to Grow and Change

Your protagonist can't change unless he first knows *how* to change. The First Act is the place to begin foreshadowing that change by giving the character a hint or two about the nature of his Lie and—even more specifically—the Truth he'll need to learn in order to counteract it.

Note: this beat doesn't necessarily mean your protagonist must *take* the first step in changing. This is still the First Act, after all, and he is still a long way from even being able to admit he has a problem. However, that doesn't mean you can't start laying the groundwork.

> **For Example:** In *What About Bob?*, Bob's cure (love and family) are strongly foreshadowed through his immediate connection with Leo's family photographs.

4. Give the Character an Inciting Event to Refuse

Think of the Inciting Event as an opportunity for your character. On the surface, it may be something awful (like a declaration of war). But for your unwitting hero, it's the opportunity he's been waiting for. He doesn't know it yet, but this is his big chance to change his life and get out from under that Lie forever. In *Plot vs. Character*, Jeff Gerke stresses,

> Good inciting events at first appear to be bothers out of the blue, but they end up being individually tailored for the hero.

Here's the important thing about the Inciting Event: Your character doesn't much like it. He considers it, then shakes his head and sticks up his nose. Nope, not interested. He's got better things to do—like polishing up his Lie. If he engages with the Inciting Event, his old life will change, and he doesn't want that. As uncomfortable as his old life may be, he'd still rather cling to its familiarity.

But it's too late! The Inciting Event has already changed the character. In ever so small a way, it has changed his awareness of himself, his world, and his problem. For the first time, he begins to realize he *has* a problem. He probably won't be able to name that problem just yet. But suddenly he's got an itch. The familiarity of his old world isn't quite so comfortable anymore.

The sturdiest timing for your story's Inciting Event is half-way through the First Act. This gives you the opportunity to introduce your character and his world before hitting him with his first major encounter with the main conflict. However, this does *not* mean the story's previous events will be unrelated to the main plot. Everything builds into everything—if only through foreshadowing.

> **For Example:** In *Jurassic Park*, Alan Grant's first response to John Hammond's preposterous offer (that Dr. Grant postpone his dig and come "pen a wee testimonial" for Hammond's theme park) is to turn him down flat. Although he gets over it quickly enough when Hammond raises the stakes, his initial reluctance is important to the story's emotional pacing.

5. Evolve the Character's Belief in the Lie

Toward the end of the First Act, the character will still be entrenched in the Lie. He believes in it just as strongly now as he did at the beginning of the story. But on a subconscious level, he is beginning to fight against its foundation. As a result, his belief in how he serves the Lie begins to evolve. If his Lie is that his worth is found in his ability to earn obscene amounts of money, then he may now begin believing that at least he should be able to gain that money honestly instead of working as a con man.

> **For Example:** At the end of her First Act, Jane Eyre still believes she must serve to be worthy of love. But now she decides she'd rather strike out on her own and take service as a governess, instead of continuing to drudge as a teacher at Lowood School for Girls.

6. Make the Character Decide

The First Act ends when the character makes a decision. He

decides to do something about that annoying Inciting Event that bumped into his life a few chapters back. In essence, he is deciding to step through the doorway between worlds. He's about to leave his Normal World (perhaps literally, perhaps metaphorically) and enter a brand new world of adventure, full of challenges he's never before faced and which he will never again be the same after having overcome. This will propel him into the First Plot Point, which we'll discuss in the next chapter.

> **For Example:** At the end of the First Act in *Secondhand Lions*, Walter decides to give up on running away and instead return to live with his uncles. This isn't a passive decision; it's an active choice, which now makes him a willing resident on the farm for the first time in the story.

FURTHER EXAMPLES OF CHARACTER ARC IN THE FIRST ACT

> *A Christmas Carol*: Scrooge's Lie is reinforced throughout the First Act in a series of encounters, first with his nephew Fred and his employee Bob Cratchit, then with the men collecting for the poor, the carolers, and, finally and most dramatically, with the ghost of Jacob Marley. We see the tiniest glimmer of a possibility for change in the real warmth of friendship that momentarily springs up in Scrooge in response to Marley. As for Marley, he doesn't just hint at what Scrooge needs to do to change; he spells it out in gory detail. Marley's warning is the Inciting Event, which Scrooge scoffs at, even in the light of such convincing proof as a real live ghost. Still, he is shaken, and a small part of his brain begins to wonder if Marley's promise of damnation might be true. He decides to stay awake until after the prophesied hour of the first ghost—just to prove to himself how crazy the whole thing is.

> *Cars*: Lightning McQueen's Lie is set up in the lengthy opening race sequence, then reinforced consistently by

his attitude throughout the First Act. We see a glimmer of hope for him in his friendship (such as it is) with his transport truck Mack, the only team member he doesn't seem to resent. Racing legend The King spells out the advice Lightning needs to hear about getting himself a "good team"—even though Lightning mostly tunes it out. The announcement of the tie-breaker race, to be held in California, is the Inciting Event. Lightning embraces it wholeheartedly, but, without yet knowing it, he simultaneously rejects the "adventure world" he's about to land in, when he scorns his rundown Rust-eze sponsors. Lightning decides to travel all night to reach California in time to schmooze the new sponsor he hopes to gain.

QUESTIONS TO ASK ABOUT YOUR CHARACTER'S ARC IN THE FIRST ACT

1. How will you introduce and reinforce your character's Lie in the First Act?

2. How will you use the "elbow room" in the First Act to space out the various layers of your character's Lie, goals, and personality?

3. How will you indicate your character's latent potential to overcome the Lie?

4. What aspect of the Truth can you share with the character in the First Act? How will you share it (through another character's mentoring, etc.)?

5. What will be your Inciting Event?

6. Why will your character initially reject the Inciting Event?

7. How quickly will your character get over his initial rejection of the Inciting Event's "call to adventure"?

8. Toward the end of the First Act, how will your character's belief in how he serves the Lie begin to evolve?

9. What decision will the character make that will engage him in the Inciting Event?

As the first building block in your character's arc, the First Act is your opportunity to lay a solid foundation for your entire story. Setup is more than half the battle. If you get everything in place in the beginning, you'll have all the tools you need at your disposal in the remaining acts. Engage your readers and launch your character on the adventure that will change his life forever.

"...many had found, or were finding,
that the point of no return
was not necessarily the edge of the precipice:
it could be the bottom of the valley,
the beginning of the long climb up the far slope,
and when a man had once begun that climb
he never looked back to that other side."
—Alistair MacLean

7

THE FIRST PLOT POINT

I F THE FIRST Act is setup, then the First Plot Point is the point of no return. This is where the setup ends, and the story begins "for real." At this point, the character commits—usually because he has no choice—to a decision that will propel him out of the comfortable stagnation of the Normal World and the Lie He Believes.

Visualize a locked door separating the First Act from the Second Act. The First Plot Point is where the protagonist sticks his key in that door and unlocks it. And like Pandora's box, he ain't never going to get it shut again.

- The First Plot Point belongs around the 20-25% mark.
- The First Plot Point ends the setup of your First Act.
- The First Plot Point is where your character leaves his Normal World.
- The First Plot Point either incorporates or is directly followed by the character's decision to react in a strong and irrevocable way.
- The First Plot Point will usually be a major scene. In a thriller or action story, something's going to explode. In a romance, this may be where the leads go out for the first time.

Whatever event your story demands, take advantage of the

opportunity to make this one of its most exciting and memorable sequences.

THE FIRST PLOT POINT

The First Plot Point will almost always be forced upon your character. Something big and unforeseen smacks him upside the head. It could be something that seems pretty good: graduating (Orson Scott Card's *Ender's Game*), digging an escape tunnel (*The Great Escape*), discovering a princess in your bedroom (William Wyler's *Roman Holiday*). But likely, it will be disastrous: a murder (Ridley Scott's *Gladiator*), a nervous breakdown (*The Kid*), a dashing of dreams (*It's a Wonderful Life*).

Whatever the manifestation, the First Plot Point's effect on your character's arc can be found in three important decisions your character must make.

Character Decision #1: *Prior to* the First Plot Point

Your First Plot Point needs to be preceded by a strong decision on your character's part (Dorothy Gale decides to run away from home; Jane Eyre decides to hire out as a governess). This decision leads the character to the First Plot Point, but the decision itself isn't the plot point. (Refer back to Part 6 of the last chapter for more info on this decision.)

The First Plot Point is then something that *happens* to your character to upend his plans (landing in Oz; meeting Rochester). It knocks his world off kilter and shakes his equilibrium all to smithereens. It either flat-out destroys his Normal World, leaving him with no choice but to physically travel on (the burning of the plantation in *The Patriot*) or it warps the Normal World, forcing the protagonist to adapt to new ways of surviving within it (the death of Uncle Ben in *Spider-Man*).

Character Decision #2: *During* the First Plot Point

The most important thing about the First Plot Point is your character's *reaction* to it. If he just stands there observing, then turns and goes back to his old life, there can be no story. The First Plot Point sets up the series of reactions that will occupy your character for the next quarter of the book, up until the Midpoint.

As such, the First Plot Point must cause one very specific initial reaction. Basically, this is just your character's decision *to* react. It's his decision to go ahead and unlock the door to the Second Act. He doesn't turn away from the First Plot Point—he moves into it.

Character Decision #3: *After* the First Plot Point

Your character will have two basic responses to the First Plot Point. Either he'll be, "Heck, yeah!"—and charge right on through that door, with no clear idea what he's really getting himself into. Or he'll be kicking and screaming as events beyond his control *drag* him through.

Either way, what's important is that the character quickly establishes a clear physical goal—based on the Thing He Wants. Usually, this goal will be very clear in relation to whatever's just happened to him at the First Plot Point. Physically, he'll have immediate needs that must be met, either in an effort to restore the old "normal" and/or in an effort to find a new normal (as will always be the case when the First Plot Point moves the character to a new setting).

This is the moment when the plot goal fully solidifies. This plot goal will propel your conflict for the rest of the story, until your character either achieves it or decides it was the wrong goal (in which case, he may or may not still physically achieve it).

Just as importantly, this definitive reaction to the First Plot Point will shape your character's arc. You know you've found the right First Plot Point when it drags your character out of his former complacency and puts his feet on the path toward destroying his Lie—even though he probably won't realize that's what's happening and, indeed, may be actively fighting that destination. Whether he realizes it or not, he has committed himself to change, even though he may still be trying to change in the *wrong* way.

The difference now is that, unlike his comfy Normal World where living by the Lie was *de rigueur*, his post-First Plot Point life will no longer enable his complacency.

How Does the First Plot Point Manifest in Character Arcs?

Your character's arc in the First Plot Point could manifest as:

Thor: Getting tossed out of his majestic Normal World because his Lie has made him too obnoxious—which gives Thor the new plot goal of trying to return to the Normal World.

Jane Eyre: Getting hired as a governess by a formidable new employer—which gives Jane the new plot goal of making both the job and the relationship work.

Jurassic Park: Arriving at the park and seeing real live dinosaurs for the first time—which gives Dr. Grant the new plot goal of exploring every inch of the park.

Secondhand Lions: Discovering Uncle Hub sword fighting in his sleep and hearing the first of Uncle Garth's stories about their youthful exploits—which gives Walter the new plot goal of learning everything he can about the mysterious Jasmine.

Toy Story: Getting (literally) kicked out of his place of honor by the arrival of the new Buzz Lightyear toy—which gives Woody the new plot goal of trying to regain his top-dog spot.

Three Kings: Discovering a map to Iraqi gold bullion—which gives Archie the new plot goal of finding the treasure.

Green Street Hooligans: Getting caught in the violent crossfire between two rival football firms (gangs)—which gives Matt the new plot goal of fighting with the firm that saves him.

What About Bob?: Traveling to Lake Winnipesaukee to find his psychiatrist—which gives Bob the new plot goal of taking a vacation from his problems.

FURTHER EXAMPLES OF THE FIRST PLOT POINT IN CHARACTER ARCS

A Christmas Carol: The Ghost of Christmas Past shows up in Scrooge's bedroom, forever changing Scrooge's perception of the world. Even if the ghost should disappear at this point, Scrooge's Normal World has been forever shaken. But the ghost doesn't disappear. Rather, it drags Scrooge through the doorway at the end of the First Act and into the Second Act. It forces Scrooge to begin the Second Act with the new plot goal of learning all he can about his own life and the Spirit of Christmas—even though Scrooge doesn't yet fully realize that is what's going on. At first, Scrooge's only goal is to survive the night. But he's already passed his point of no return: he can never go back to his Normal World. The world itself hasn't changed, but he has.

Cars: The Thing Lightning McQueen Wants (the Piston Cup) is dragged out of his immediate reach when he is accidentally marooned—and arrested—in the forgotten rural town of Radiator Springs. He had no desire or intention to venture out of his glittering Normal World, and his immediate reaction to the First Plot Point is to form the plot goal of getting his bumper back to Normal as fast as he can rev his engine. But in this new world, all the rules are different. The Lie-spawned behavior he's been rewarded for previously now gets him into deeper and deeper trouble in Radiator Springs.

QUESTIONS TO ASK ABOUT THE FIRST PLOT POINT IN YOUR CHARACTER'S ARC

1. What major event will slam into your character's Normal World and force him to alter his original plans?

2. What decision will lead your protagonist to the First Plot Point?

3. Will the First Plot Point *seem* favorable? If so, how will the complications turn out to be worse than the protagonist expected?

4. Or will this event be obviously disastrous? How?

5. Will the protagonist willingly embrace the First Plot Point and walk into the Second Act under his own power?

6. Or will he have to be dragged, kicking and screaming, through the gateway between acts?

7. Will the First Plot Point destroy the Normal World? Or will it physically remove your character from the Normal World? Or will it warp the Normal World *around* the protagonist?

8. How will your character react to the First Plot Point?

9. What new plot goal will the character form in response to the First Plot Point?

10. How will the First Plot Point put your character's feet on the path to his new Truth?

11. How will the First Plot Point create a new world in which the character will be "punished" for acting according to his Lie?

The First Act is about setting up your character's Lie. From the First Plot Point on, that Lie's days are numbered. From here on out, the Second Act is about destroying the Lie and helping the character find the Truth that will allow him to combat the external conflict and grow into a whole person. Plan a First Plot Point that will tear away your character's safety nets and force him to step out into the biggest adventure of his life!

"There are two ways to be fooled.
One is to believe what isn't true;
the other is to refuse to believe what is true."
—Søren Kierkegaard

8

THE FIRST HALF OF THE
SECOND ACT

I N THE STRUCTURE of character arcs, the First Half
of the Second Act is where your character ventures (or is
thrust) into uncharted territory—and gets lost. He may not
quite see it that way himself, but this is where he begins to discover that the old rules (the Lie He Believes) no longer apply.

This puts him in a bit of a tailspin. He scrambles to react to
the events of the First Plot Point, while chasing as hard as ever
after the Thing He Wants. He's reactive in the sense that he's
at the mercy of the antagonistic force; he is not in control of
the conflict. But don't confuse reactivity with passivity. Your
character will be *very* active in his pursuit of his goals during
this time, and he'll be learning which methods of achieving
that goal are ineffective. This new knowledge will, in turn, lay
the groundwork for helping him begin to realize how his belief
in the Lie is holding him back.

The Second Act is the largest section of your story, com-
prising roughly 50%—which is why I like to break it down into
three parts: the First Half of the Second Act, the Midpoint,
and the Second Half of the Second Act. We'll discuss the Midpoint and the Second Half in future chapters.

The First Half of the Second Act is where your character
reacts to the First Plot Point.

The First Half of the Second Act shows your character trying to regain his balance and figure out how to survive in this new world in which he finds himself.

The First Half of the Second Act features a Pinch Point (at the 37% mark), in which the antagonist flexes his muscles and reminds readers what the protagonist is up against.

The First Half of the Second Act begins immediately after the First Plot Point and continues until the Midpoint at the 50% mark.

Speaking generally, you can divide your book into two halves. The first half is about the character's reacting to events; the second is about his taking action. This is nowhere clearer than in the First Half of the Second Act, as the true burden of the character's Lie finally begins to emerge.

4 Parts of the Character Arc in the First Half of the Second Act

As you structure your character's arc in the First Half of the Second Act, be sure to incorporate the following four landmarks. There is no firm timing for any of these; as long as they take place before the Midpoint, you'll have everything in place for the next big turning point in your character's development.

1. Provide the Character With Tools to Overcome His Lie

After the First Plot Point shakes up your character's Normal World, he's going to be in a vulnerable state—which means he's primed to receive help in overcoming his Lie. He won't be given all the tools yet, but he will receive at least a nail. He will receive one piece of the puzzle. Or you might think of it as the first rung of the ladder he will use to scale the wall of the Lie.

This first tool will come in the form of information on how to overcome the Lie. Often, it will result from another character (often a Mentor or Guardian archetype) offering advice. At the same time as he's learning necessary physical skills to battle the antagonist in the Climax, he should also be learning Truths to combat his Lie.

These truths should be more than just theoretical; they need to be applicable truths. For instance, if your character's Lie is *he travels fastest who travels alone*, then the tools he's receiving in this section shouldn't be just someone else *telling* him, *many hands make light work*. Rather, he should be given practicable opportunities to learn the Truth by seeing it in action. In other words, *show, don't tell*.

> **For Example:** In *Toy Story*, Bo Peep encourages a marginalized (and slightly hysterical) Woody by telling him, "I know Andy's excited about Buzz, but you know he'll always have a special place for you."

2. Show the Protagonist Encountering Difficulties in Pursuing His Lie

As of the First Plot Point, the world around the protagonist has changed. But he still hasn't caught up. The light of Truth may be glimmering at the edge of his vision, but he isn't consciously aware of it yet. He has yet to even recognize there *is* a Lie to overcome. He's still trying to pursue business as usual. He's reacting to new events in the same ol' way—and it's not working.

Throughout the Second Act, the character will be, in essence, punished for acting according to his Lie. Where before his Lie seemed to empower him and get him what he wanted, his Lie now begins to increasingly get in his way. It's becoming a stumbling block in his progress toward, not just the Thing He Needs, but even the Thing He Wants—and, by extension, his overall plot goal. He persists in his Lie-based actions, simply because he doesn't yet realize what's going on, and he is "punished" for it.

As a result of this punishment, the character will begin to evolve his tactics. Even though he may not yet be able to recognize the underlying Lie that's causing his failures, he *will* recognize he's failing. He'll start seeking out ways to adapt his behavior.

> **For Example:** After Thor finds himself banished to Earth, his old attitude as an arrogant immortal has him attempting to muscle his way to authority—and failing in a variety of humiliating ways (getting tasered, sedated, and run over).

3. Move the Character Closer to What He Wants and Farther From What He Needs

At this point, the character is still hellbent on getting his hands on the Thing He Wants. Because he's convinced it's going to solve all his problems, he desires it with a single-minded fanaticism. However, what he fails to realize as he races toward his goal is that the closer he gets to the Thing He Wants, the farther it's pushing him away from the Thing He Needs.

Despite the problems engendered by his faulty, Lie-based methods, your character will still be making definite progress toward his goal in this section. In *The Kid*, Russ seems to have gotten rid of his young doppelganger. In *Monsters, Inc.*, Sully and Mike have a plan for sending Boo home. In Ernest Cline's *Ready Player One*, Wade is leading the scoreboard and winning the girl.

But these seeming advances are just whitewash on top of worm-eaten wood. These surface victories are blinding the character to the true nature of his inner conflict. The lure of the Thing He Wants is pulling him toward his destruction. He may be on his way to succeeding in the outer conflict, but, if he keeps heading down this path, he's destined to lose his inner battle.

> **For Example:** In *Three Kings*, the characters find the gold, steal it, and head out of town. They've got what they want, but they're leaving an entire village at the mercy of enemy soldiers, making them no better than the men they've risked their lives fighting.

4. Give the Character a Glimpse of Life Without the Lie

The First Plot Point sets up a brand-new scenario for the character—one in which he glimpses, for the first time, what life might be like without the Lie. This glimpse will probably result from a demonstration of other characters' actions and attitudes, but it could also come thanks to the character's momentarily shedding his Lie and getting a hint of the reward of Truth.

At this early stage in the story, the character shouldn't get much *more* than a glimpse. But even though he's not yet ready to be convinced of the faulty premise of his Lie, he should begin to see the cracks. There's life beyond the Lie, and it's a pretty awesome life. He needs to be given just the smallest sense of how great it would feel to cast aside the Lie and never look back.

For Example: In *Green Street Hooligans*, Matt fights alongside his brother-in-law's football firm and learns, for the first time, how good it feels to fight back when someone pushes you around.

FURTHER EXAMPLES OF CHARACTER ARC IN THE FIRST HALF OF THE SECOND ACT

A Christmas Carol: The three spirits provide Scrooge with tool after tool to overcome his Lie. The Ghost of Christmas Past walks him through his history, reminding him of wonderful memories from his young manhood working at Old Fezziwig's. The ghost gets Scrooge to admit that Fezziwig's kindness made Fezziwig a bigger man than any amount of money could have. The ghost then shows Scrooge a glimpse of what his life *might* have been had he rejected the Lie from the outset and married Belle. Scrooge resists the revelations and wrestles with the ghost, only to have it dump him back in his house—and into the lap of another spirit.

Cars: Lightning McQueen receives tools from just about every character he meets in Radiator Springs. Mater and Miss Sally talk about how wonderful Radiator Springs is, with its friendly neighbors and leisurely pace of living. But he resists. He scares off their customers by trying to escape his community service sentence, and Doc "punishes" him by challenging him to race—and beating him. Lightning tries to move toward the Thing He Wants and away from Radiator Springs by fixing the road as fast as possible. Throughout the First Half of the Second Act, the townsfolk keep showing him a world where people care for each other. The Truth is right in front of Lightning's face, but he keeps resisting it, insisting it doesn't even appeal to him.

QUESTIONS TO ASK ABOUT YOUR CHARACTER'S ARC IN THE FIRST HALF OF THE SECOND ACT

1. How is your character reacting to the First Plot Point?

2. What "tools" can you provide to help your character build the first rung in the ladder that will scale his Lie?

3. What minor character can offer advice or exemplary behavior to help mentor your protagonist?

4. How can you *show* the protagonist the first step in overcoming his Lie, instead of just *telling* him about it?

5. How will your character attempt to use his Lie to solve plot problems?

6. How will he be "punished" as a result?

7. How will these failures evolve your character's outlook and tactics?

8. How will your character's single-minded pursuit of his plot goal lead him closer to the Thing He Wants?

9. How will his pursuit of the Thing He Wants cause him to risk turning farther away from the Thing He Needs?

10. After the First Plot Point, how will the new world or the altered Normal World provide the character with a glimpse of how life might be without his Lie?

During the First Half of the Second Act, your character will be more determined than ever to reach his plot goal. He's trying very hard to take control of his life—and the conflict—and, on some levels, it totally seems to be working. On other levels, however, he's messing up worse than ever.

Use the First Half of the Second Act to explore the depths of your character's personality, beliefs, and desires. The result is a well of endless possibilities for fun, conflict-powered scenes!

"Human identity is
the most fragile thing that we have,
and it's often only found in moments of truth."
—Alan Rudolph

9

THE MIDPOINT

I N A POSITIVE Change Arc, your protagonist will have spent the First Half of the Second Act blundering around in foreign territory, making mistakes based on false assumptions, and getting his hand slapped for his every wrong move. But he's also going to have been slowly—maybe even subconsciously—learning his lesson and figuring things out. These personal revelations are going to lead him up to a very special turning point at the story's Midpoint, 50% of the way into the story.

Up to now, your protagonist will have been struggling under the burden of his Lie. He's still overwhelmingly convinced he can't possibly live without it. But the First Half of the Second Act has altered him, probably without his even realizing it. He's ready for a big change. The Midpoint is that change. It prompts the character to turn away from the *effects* of the Lie, if not the Lie itself quite yet.

The Midpoint acts as the swivel for the entire story. Not only is it a crucial moment of revelation in your character's arc, it also marks the end of his reactive phase and his transition into active mode.

Director Sam Peckinpah referred to the Midpoint as a story's "centerpiece": it's big, impressive, and the center of attention. Your Midpoint is an important opportunity for a killer scene. In his book *Write Your Novel From the Middle*, James Scott Bell recommends starting your plotting with your Midpoint, so you can plan your entire story around this moment.

THE MIDPOINT

In discussions of plot structure, the Midpoint's emphasis is always placed on the protagonist's shift from a reactive role (*not* in control of the conflict) to an active role (taking control of the conflict). This is the fundamental turning point in your book. Without this shift, you have no evolution, no variety, and no story.

But taken at face value, this explanation of the Midpoint is incomplete. Where, after all, does this shift come from?

It comes from deep inside the character. It comes from the heart of his character arc.

The Moment of Truth

At the Midpoint, the character ceases to survive merely in a reactionary role and begins to take definitive action in overcoming the antagonistic force. He does this, not because his goal or his determination to achieve that goal have changed, but because the Midpoint is where he will gain a better understanding of both the external conflict and his inner self *in* that conflict.

In other words, he finally sees the Truth. Stanley D. Williams calls this the "moment of grace." James Scott Bell calls it the "mirror moment" (since it metaphorically—and sometimes literally—involves the character looking in a mirror and seeing the truth about himself). The character has been seeing evidence of the Truth throughout the first half of the story, but the Moment of Truth at the Midpoint is where he finally accepts that Truth. He accepts it not just as a universal, generic truth, but as a Truth that is the key to achieving his plot goal, and, by extension, the Thing He Wants.

Caught Between the Lie and the Truth

This does *not* mean the character rejects the Lie. It's still too early in the story for that. But the Midpoint shows him the importance of the opposing viewpoint. Consciously, he will continue to claim he believes the Lie throughout the rest of the Second Act, but subconsciously, he will begin to act in harmony with the Truth.

For example, the murder of Po-han at the Midpoint in Richard McKenna's *The Sand Pebbles* forces protagonist Jake Holman to face the Truth that *it's impossible to stay personally neutral while in the midst of a war*. He still claims neutrality at this point, insisting *the morality and politics of war are something for the officers to "fool with."* But his actions in plotting to desert the Navy prove that, deep in his soul, he no longer holds with that Lie of neutrality.

At this point, your character is now a divided person: caught between the Lie and the Truth. His incomplete understanding of how to *implement* his new knowledge of the Truth is the reason he will not yet be able to achieve total victory in the remainder of the Second Act.

Part of a Subtle Evolution

Although the Midpoint itself will be part of a big and important series of scenes, the character's personal shift from Lie to Truth will often be a subtle moment. He may not be able to consciously articulate the change, but the change itself will nonetheless be solid and dramatic. In *The Moral Premise*, Williams writes:

> The Moment of Grace is usually triggered by a subtle event that is undergirded by earlier, more dramatic events. It is not the Moment of Grace alone that changes the character's behavior, but it is the "straw that breaks the camel's back."

How Does the Midpoint Manifest in Character Arcs?

Your character's arc in the Midpoint could manifest as:

Thor: A physical inability to lift his own hammer—and a realization that *strength alone does not make Thor worthy* to wield it.

Jane Eyre: A glimpse into *the horror of Rochester's secret and his growing dependence upon Jane*—and a realization that she cannot continue to work for him if he is to marry someone else.

***Jurassic Park*:** A stunning attack upon the children by the T-Rex, now loose from her pen—and a realization that *the children must be rescued, even at the risk of Dr. Grant's own life.*

***Secondhand Lions*:** A brawl between Uncle Hub and a greaser gang—and the realization that *Uncle Garth's heroic stories may be true after all.*

***Toy Story*:** A jealousy-fueled assault on Buzz that ends with both of them abandoned at a gas station—and the realization that *Woody can't return to Andy if he doesn't save Buzz too.*

***Three Kings*:** The discovery and theft of the sought-after Iraqi gold—and the realization *Archie and the others can't leave the Shiite villagers to face the consequences.*

***Green Street Hooligans*:** A victorious fight at the Manchester game—and the realization of *the empowerment of being able to fight with and for people Matt cares about.*

***What About Bob?*:** A successful (if somewhat accidental) diving lesson with Dr. Leo's son—and the realization that *"the fam" are subsequently paying attention to Bob because they like him, not because he's crazy.*

FURTHER EXAMPLES OF THE MIDPOINT IN CHARACTER ARCS

***A Christmas Carol*:** After an eventful First Half of the Second Act, spent exploring his past, Scrooge is passed into the hands of the second spirit, the Ghost of Christmas Present. Scrooge is already comparatively subdued by this point, not even daring to meet the ghost's eyes. The First Act has shaken his belief in his Lie of *money's absolute worth,* and everything he has witnessed has convinced him maybe he does have something to learn about being a better man. He humbly submits to the ghost's powers and admits he has "learned a lesson which is working on me now." He's not quite ready to completely surrender his Lie, but the Truth now has him in its grip. His Moment of Truth manifests when he not only doesn't resist this ghost, as he did the first one, but even entreats him, "Tonight, if you have aught to teach me, let me profit by it."

Cars: After losing the race to Doc, Lightning still believes just as firmly as ever that he works best "solo mio." But he is now confronted with the Truth that *he needs help*. He can't figure out how to make the turn on the dirt racetrack without Doc's advice. He doesn't want to admit that Truth, but, deep down, he can't escape it. He goes tractor tipping with Mater and has to admit to himself that he likes Mater and has fun with him. His Moment of Truth sneaks up on him when he starts complaining about his Rust-eze sponsors, only to realize he's also criticizing Mater. Miss Sally emphasizes the new Truth by reminding him that Mater trusts him and that, *in having a friend he can trust, he must now be trustworthy himself*. Lightning responds nonchalantly, but his actions in helping the town in the second half will bear out that, in his heart, he believes this new Truth.

QUESTIONS TO ASK ABOUT YOUR CHARACTER'S ARC IN THE MIDPOINT

1. What personal revelation strikes your protagonist at the Midpoint?

2. How is your protagonist different at the Midpoint from who he was at the First Plot Point?

3. How does the revelation at the Midpoint prompt the character to move from reaction to action by providing him the knowledge to start taking control of the conflict?

4. What definitive action will your protagonist take against the antagonistic force?

5. What new understanding of the conflict does the protagonist gain at the Midpoint?

6. What new understanding of himself does the protagonist gain at the Midpoint?

7. What is his Moment of Truth? What Truth does he recognize and accept? What causes him to accept it?

8. How is your character still consciously clinging to his Lie?

9. What actions is he taking that are based on the Truth?

10. How does the contrast between the simultaneously held Lie and Truth evolve his inner conflict?

The Midpoint is one of the most exciting moments in your story. It's the moment your character finally *gets it.* The puzzle pieces fall into place. He realizes what he must do to win the conflict, and he adjusts his actions accordingly. This isn't an overnight transformation. It's a build-up of everything he's learned in the First Act, and he will continue to refine his understanding of the Truth throughout the remainder of the Second Act.

When planning your Midpoint, identify the Truth your character must recognize and create a mind-blowing scene to support it. Done right, it will end up being one of the most memorable chapters in your entire book.

"We have walked through
the darkness of this world,
that's why we are able to see
even a sliver of light."
—Masashi Kishimoto

10

THE SECOND HALF OF THE SECOND ACT

THE SECOND HALF of the Second Act is where you cue the hero music in character arcs. Thanks to that major personal revelation at the Midpoint, the protagonist now *gets it*. The puzzle pieces are falling into place. The light bulbs have flashed on. He sees what he has to do to win the conflict. Bad guys, watch out!

The Second Half of the Second Act is where your character shifts out of the reactive phase (in which the conflict is being controlled by the antagonist) and moves into the active phase (in which he starts taking control of the conflict for himself). He learned the Truth at the Midpoint, and it is allowing him to start implementing the correct actions to get the desired results in his quest for the plot goal.

Sounds like the story's already all wrapped up, doesn't it? After all, that's what your hero's starting to believe.

But not so fast, Buster Brown!

This story ain't over, not by a long shot. And all those lessons your protagonist thinks he's now got a handle on? Well, turns out he's only got *half* a handle on them. He may have figured out the Truth, but he still hasn't relinquished his Lie—and that Lie is still the crux of the problem.

The Second Half of the Second Act begins with a strong action from the protagonist, based on his Midpoint revelation.

The Second Half of the Second Act features your character moving forward confidently, taking control of the conflict.

The Second Half of the Second Act is where you need to assemble all your story's playing pieces, so they're in place for the Third Act.

The Second Half of the Second Act begins with the Midpoint and spans 25% of the book to the beginning of the Third Act at the 75% mark.

The Second Half of the Second Act features a Second Pinch Point (at the 62% mark), which emphasizes the antagonist's ability to defeat the protagonist and foreshadows the final battle.

Speaking generally, the Second Half of the Second Act is the "action" phase. The protagonist charges ahead, *thinking* he now sees clearly. But the key thing to remember about this section of the story is that your character is still half-blinded by the Lie. He's charging into the conflict, thinking he now has 20/20 vision, when, really, he only has one eye open.

6 PARTS OF THE CHARACTER ARC IN THE SECOND HALF OF THE SECOND ACT

We have six important elements to discuss about the Second Half of the Second Act. With a few exceptions (noted below), you have a lot of flexibility in how you place these elements within the Second Half of the Second Act. Pacing will be your major consideration. As long as you've set up all these elements before the Third Plot Point, you'll have everything properly in place for the big show in the Climax.

1. Allow the Character to Act in Enlightened Ways

Thanks to the lessons learned in the First Half of the Second Act and the revelation at the Midpoint, the character is now able to act in ways he wouldn't have been able to in the first half.

Specifically, this means he now has new tools to work with, which will allow him to make significant progress toward the Thing He Wants. Before, he may have been trying to tear down the brick wall between him and his goal by using his fingernails to pry bricks loose. Now, however, he has a pickax—and, even better, the knowledge of which bricks he needs to shatter in order to bring the whole wall crashing down.

Now your character can start moving past obstacles with greater speed. This does *not* mean his progress is unimpeded, but because he now seems to be on the right track, he's much more efficient at eliminating or sidestepping the obstacles.

> **For Example:** In *What About Bob?*, being accepted by Leo's family has empowered Bob, and he starts to come alive in the Second Half of the Second Act, as he charismatically salvages Leo's disastrous *Good Morning America* interview, then charms the staff at the psychiatric hospital after Leo tries to involuntarily commit him.

2. Trap the Character Between the Old Lie and the New Truth

Possibly *the most important thing* to understand about this section of the story is that the character has not yet relinquished his Lie. The Midpoint has brought him to an understanding of the Truth, and he is busy acting on it. But he has yet to face the Lie. It's still there, buried deep inside his subconscious.

And the result is cognitive dissonance. He's trapped between two incompatible beliefs. This will cause him to make mistakes. He believes in the Truth; he's acting on the Truth. But he's not yet 100% committed to it. The Lie is holding him back, and it's causing him some pretty severe inner conflict. One minute he acts on the Truth; the next, the Lie rears its warty head, and he tries to act on it instead.

In *Plot vs. Character*, Jeff Gerke calls this "vacillation escalation":

> You see the key element here, right? Vacillation. That doesn't mean the character is weak minded. It just means that where there was once only one power in the character's quadrant of the universe, now there are two [the Truth and the Lie—the right way and the wrong way]. Everything isn't as settled as the hero once thought.

For Example: In *Toy Story*, Woody has committed to the Truth that *he must rescue Buzz if he's to return to Andy*. But the Lie that fuels his jealousy and hatred of Buzz is still alive and well. He's not helping Buzz because he wants to; he's helping him because he has to. He drags Buzz along without ever stopping to consider him as an equal or to wonder what's up with his sudden change in personality after Buzz sees the toy commercial on TV. Woody's Lie continues to get in his way, even as the Truth enables him to make decided progress toward his goal.

3. Initiate the Character's Attempts to Escape the *Effects* of the Lie

The character is starting to feel more and more uncomfortable with the Lie's *effects* in his life. The Truth is seducing him in all its sparkly glory. He *wants* the Truth. So he starts moving toward it. It's sucking him in, like a tractor beam. The Lie keeps swarming around his head, darting at his face like a mosquito. But he's entranced by the Truth. He keeps walking toward it, batting the Lie away again and again.

At this point, if someone asked him if he still believed the Lie, he would reflexively insist, "Of course I do!" But his actions are starting to tell a different story. He's so drawn to the Truth that, in moving toward it (and the Thing He Needs), he may even be moving *away* from the Thing He Wants. Often, this can be seen when a character begins to act more selflessly in the Second Half. He still wants whatever it is he Wants, but he's so busy doing what's right that the Thing He Wants gets shoved to the back burner.

For Example: In *Three Kings*, the characters still *want* the gold. They're just as determined as ever to smuggle every last brick back to the States. But their actions now have an entirely different focus: they're committed to helping the Shiite villagers get across the border to safety *before* they go back for their gold.

4. Contrast Your Character's "Before and After" Mindsets

We can think of the two halves of a story as mirror images of each other. Throughout the second half, the character should be put in situations that reflect back upon those in the first half. The only difference? They're *reverse* images.

Think of these as "before and after" scenes. By purposefully placing the character in a second-half scene that is similar to a first-half scene, you're able to give readers a dramatic representation of the progress he's made in his personal evolution. In the first half, he was a selfish jerk who threw his fast food garbage at the homeless guy on the corner; in the second half, he looks at the guy, looks at his uneaten Big Mac—and hands it over.

Your character is a different person in the Second Half of the Second Act. Prove it. Don't just tell readers he's different. Show them.

> **For Example:** In his First Act, Thor wantonly and carelessly plunges his friends into battle and nearly gets them killed. In the Second Act, when they risk a journey to Earth to rescue him, he expresses his gratefulness to see them again but tells them they should not have endangered themselves for him. He proves how his "always attack" mindset in the first half has evolved when he admits the (comparative) weakness of his mortal body and chooses to help evacuate the townspeople rather than join the fight with his friends.

5. Provide Your Character With a False Victory

Thanks to your character's energetic and enlightened determination in this section, the Second Act will end with what, at first glance, appears to be a great big victory. The Thing He Wants will seem to be right within his grasp. All he has to do is reach out and take it.

But that inner conflict boils up more insistently than ever. The Thing He Wants is *right there*. And, by golly, he still wants it with everything that's in him. But he's unsettled. Something about the whole thing doesn't feel right.

If he's going to claim the Thing He Wants under these circumstances, he will have to subject himself to the Lie's thrall once again. He will have to sacrifice the Thing He Needs and stifle the call of the Truth. Is it worth it? After all, he's been after the Thing He Wants ever since the beginning of the story. And here it is—his for the taking.

So what does he do?

He *takes* it. He convinces himself the Thing He Wants is not an obstacle to the Thing He Needs. He can have the best of both worlds. Surely, the Lie and the Truth can live in harmony within him. So he grabs the Thing He Wants, and the conflict seems, if not won, then at least within sight of a victory.

However, as the Third Plot Point will prove, his peace is a false one. He's sacrificed his deeper inner Need to gain a physical victory, and you gotta know he's going to have to pay for that one.

> **For Example:** Jane Eyre seems to get exactly what she wants when she agrees to marry Rochester. She's found someone she loves who adores her back. She never expected to be loved, and yet, out of the clear blue sky, all her wildest dreams are about to come true. Of course, she says *yes!* But inside, she's not at peace. She senses, almost right away, that in marrying Rochester, she is once again sacrificing her independence of spirit and enslaving herself. She wants to be with him so much she throws the Truth right back out the window and clings to the Lie that *emotional and physical servitude have to be the price for love.*

6. Blatantly Demonstrate the Crux of Your Character's Arc

Subtlety is one of the writer's greatest weapons. But now is not the time for subtlety. Now is the time to bring out the big guns. Right before hurling your character into the maw of his personal crucible (aka the Third Act), you have to give him (and the readers) a solid validation of the Truth. Spell it out. What is the Thing He Needs?

This demonstration can come in the form of dialogue between characters, an action on the part of a character (Jane Eyre strives to gain an "independency" of money, even as she bows herself under the weight of Rochester's love), or internal narrative. Your character needs this final tool at the end of the Second Act, because, come the Third Act, it will be his first line of defense against the Lie.

> **For Example:** In *Secondhand Lions*, Uncle Hub shares with Walter a small part of the speech he likes to give young men, and it just so happens that the part he shares applies directly to Walter's fear of putting his faith in the people he loves. Hub says, "Sometimes the things that may or may not be true are the things that a man needs to believe in the most.... Doesn't matter if it's true or not. [A] man should believe in those things, because those are the things worth believing in."

FURTHER EXAMPLES OF CHARACTER ARC IN THE SECOND HALF OF THE SECOND ACT

> *A Christmas Carol*: Scrooge's mindset has notably evolved by the Second Half of the Second Act. He begins to show concern for the people who are unable to purchase bread on the Sabbath (although his logic is still misguided by his Lie). He sympathizes with Tiny Tim, and he grows "light of heart" while observing his nephew's dinner party. He would even join in their toast if he could—but, of course, he can't, because he is still physically bound by his Lie. *A Christmas Carol* is rife with "before and after" moments, sown masterfully in the First Act, and brought to fruition throughout the Second Act, as Scrooge joyfully re-encounters the people he knows and whom he treated poorly in the beginning. The story is also rife with blatant demonstrations of the thematic principle, since the tale is essentially a fable from start to finish.

Cars: After the Midpoint, Lightning's mind has been opened. He views Radiator Springs in a new light and is rewarded with discovery after discovery—Doc's three Piston Cup victories and Miss Sally's reasons for leaving behind the fast lane. Doc blatantly challenges him, "When is the last time you cared about something except yourself, hot rod? You name me one time.... These are good folk around here, who care about one another. I don't want them depending on someone they can't count on." Lightning responds with a string of genuinely kind and generous actions, first fixing the road he ruined, then visiting all the townsfolk's shops. He still wants to get to California for the tiebreaker race, but, just at the moment, he's a little distracted with how great the Truth feels here in Radiator Springs.

QUESTIONS TO ASK ABOUT YOUR CHARACTER'S ARC IN THE SECOND HALF OF THE SECOND ACT

1. How is your character starting to take control of the conflict after the Midpoint?

2. How is the revelation at the Midpoint allowing your character to see the conflict in a new light?

3. What "tools" has the Midpoint revelation given your character that make him more effective in confronting the antagonist?

4. How is your character still clinging to his Lie?

5. How is his new Truth causing friction with his old Lie?

6. How is your character still out of sync with the Truth?

7. How does your character's mindset still support the Lie?

8. How do his actions demonstrate his growing belief in the Truth?

9. How can you use a "before and after" scene to prove

how your character is different from who he was in the first half of the story?

10. What false victory will end the Second Act? How has your character compromised the Truth in order to (seemingly) gain the Thing He Wants?

11. How have you blatantly demonstrated the Truth somewhere in the Second Half of the Second Act?

On its surface, the Second Half of the Second Act will seem comparatively great for your character. Everything is going his way. He's learning the value of implementing the Truth in his life. He sees the Truth in action and begins to value it—probably without even realizing it—more than he values the Thing He Wants. Out of habit as much as anything, he's going to betray that Truth at the end of the Second Act, but he's already too far gone on the Truth to ever abandon it. He's already a changed person—and when he reaches the Third Plot Point, he'll prove it.

"The great thing about falling apart,
is that you get to decide how to
put yourself back together.
Make good choices."
—Stacie Hammond

11

THE THIRD PLOT POINT

I F YOU HAD to pick the single most important moment in a character's arc, what would it be? The Third Plot Point, you say? Well, you'd be right. Now here's the harder question: *Why* is this the most important moment?

The Third Plot Point is the low moment in your story. A minute ago, at the end of the Second Act, your protagonist seemed to have won a victory. Everything seemed to be going his way. He was getting the Truth figured out, and he seemed to have pushed the Lie to the back of his life. Even the antagonist appeared to be at his mercy.

Cue the "happily ever after" sonata, right?

Nopers. Because, as you know all too well by now, pushing that Lie to the back burner isn't good enough. Before this story can end, that Lie has to reappear front and center and confront the protagonist head on. That's what the Third Plot Point is all about. This low moment—which is all the more crushing because it comes on the heels of a seeming victory—will *force* the character to stop deceiving himself about the Lie. He can't evade it anymore. He can't pretend it away. He has to confront it once and for all—and either destroy it or be destroyed.

THE THIRD PLOT POINT

The Second Half of the Second Act was a place of empowerment for your protagonist. His embrace of the Truth after the Midpoint allowed him to act rightly with more and more conviction (and success) throughout the rest of the Second Act. But after the apparent victory that closed out the Second Act, the Third Plot Point now forces a crisis—in both the plot and the character's arc.

This point of crisis is the result of a reversal enacted by the antagonistic force. The protagonist thought he had the bad guy down for the count, but the baddie's got one more trick up his sleeve. Usually, this reversal is accompanied by a completely unexpected (although, of course, *not* unforeshadowed) revelation.

Sometimes this revelation will be a plot twist, but often it will be nothing more than a sudden and full understanding of the protagonist's Lie-empowered weaknesses. It's this new information, as much as anything, that lays your protagonist open for the final blow. He's so stunned he can't even fight back.

The Ultimate Choice Between Want and Need

In plot terms, the Third Plot Point is all about creating a "physical" moment in which the protagonist's plot goals are endangered. In character terms, the Third Plot Point hinges upon not just "something bad" happening in the outer conflict, but rather an inner choice on the protagonist's part.

At last, after two long story acts, he must *choose* between the Thing He Wants and the Thing He Needs—between the Lie and the Truth. Throughout the Second Half of the Second Act, he convinced himself he could have both. Now, he realizes that's impossible.

If this moment is to bear its full weight in the story, it must be a soul-wrenching choice. Whatever the protagonist decides here, he will lose something vital. He can either choose the Truth and lose his dream. Or he can choose his heart's desire and live the Lie for the rest of his life.

The Thing the Character Wants needs to be within his grasp. It's finally right *there*, in all its wonderful glory. He's dreamed about it for so long. Now it's his for the taking. All he has to do is close his eyes to the Truth and reach out and take it. He wants it so badly, the desire for it is practically killing him. The stronger your character's yearning for the Thing He Wants at this point, the more powerful your Third Plot Point will be.

But that's only one side of the choice. The other is the Truth—which he has also come to realize he can't live without. Even as the siren song of the Thing He Wants beckons him almost irresistibly, his eyes are finally opened to the full horror of the Lie. He shudders at the thought of sacrificing the Thing He Wants, but he is equally sickened by the possibility of having to reject the Truth and step back into the shadows of his Lie. In *Plot vs. Character*, Jeff Gerke emphasizes:

> [The protagonist] comes to understand both the promise and the price of the two ways. He comes, in other words, to truly understand his choice…. The moment … is not complete unless the hero understands not only what he stands to gain by choosing one option over the other, but also what he stands to lose.

Since this is a *Positive* Change Arc, your readers all know, deep down, what your protagonist is going to choose. However, the harder his choice, the more readers will begin to doubt his final decision—and the more powerful his choice will be when he makes it.

The Old Self Dies

Finally, his heart feeling as if it's about to tear in two, the protagonist makes his choice. He chooses *Truth*. He chooses to reject the Lie. He will not allow himself to live by this false belief anymore. He will embrace the Truth and do the right thing, even though it means (or in some stories, seems to mean) forever losing the Thing He Wants. (Whether or not he actually gains the Thing He Wants in the end is irrelevant. For now, the only thing that matters is that he is fully willing to give it up.)

At this point, the choice must become more than a decision; it must become an action. His convictions are so strong they force him to act in a way that solidifies his new path. He must burn his physical bridges. After the Third Plot Point, he won't be able to go back and change his mind in order to gain the Thing He Wants, even if his resolve should later weaken.

Metaphorically, this moment is a representation of the character's dying to his old self. Although he may still experience doubts throughout the Third Act, he is, *at this moment*, so committed to the Truth that he's willing to physically die for it. Indeed, he *does* metaphorically die right alongside his Lie.

The Third Plot Point will often feature actual death, either literally or symbolically. If an important character doesn't end up literally dying here (as, for example, Obi-Wan does in *Star Wars*), death might be represented via life-threatening weather in the background, the character losing his job (signifying professional death), a pet's death, a funeral on the road, or an obituary in the paper. The death motif *must* be organic to your story. The symbolism can never be arbitrary (e.g., the funeral the character passes on the road must have some connection to the plot). But the pall of death will almost always be, if not in the forefront, then hovering in the background of the Third Plot Point.

How Does the Third Plot Point Manifest in Character Arcs?

Your character's arc in the Third Plot Point could manifest as:

Thor: A ruthless attack on an innocent town (including people Thor has come to care about) when his brother attempts to kill him. Thor chooses to literally stop fighting and sacrifice his own life to save others.

Jane Eyre: The discovery that Rochester is already married to a madwoman and that Jane can only remain with him if she's willing to sacrifice her spiritual and moral freedom by becoming his mistress. She decides the price for being loved is too high—and flees.

Jurassic Park: The electrocution of Tim, followed by the escape of the raptors. Dr. Grant decides to do whatever he must to protect the children.

Secondhand Lions: The return of Walter's mother and her latest abusive boyfriend and their claim that his uncles are thieves who have been lying to him about how they became rich. Walter chooses to reject his mother's lies and refuses to reveal the money's whereabouts.

Toy Story: A refusal by Andy's other toys to help Woody escape Sid's room, followed by Buzz getting strapped to Sid's rocket. Woody realizes he can't escape alone and chooses to admit that Andy's need for both Woody and Buzz is more important than his own escape.

Three Kings: The realization that Troy has been captured by Iraqis and is being tortured. Archie and the Chief decide to sacrifice half their gold in a deal to get vehicles and return to save him.

Green Street Hooligans: A betrayal by one of the firm members that leads to Matt's brother-in-law being stabbed. Matt decides it's time to walk away from the violence and take his sister and her son to safety in America.

What About Bob?: The psychotic breakdown of Bob's psychiatrist. Bob chooses to heed "the fam's" wishes and leave them, even though they've all grown to care for one another.

FURTHER EXAMPLES OF THE THIRD PLOT POINT IN CHARACTER ARCS

A Christmas Carol: On the stroke of midnight, just as Jacob Marley predicted, Scrooge is visited by the most terrifying specter yet—the Ghost of Christmas Future. The stink of death is miasmic in this section. Tiny Tim's death is revealed. But, even more important, Scrooge's death and its callous treatment by acquaintances and strangers alike, fills the Third Plot Point and most of the Third Act. Scrooge clearly sees the cost of his Lie and finally decides he will surrender his wealth and live the rest of his life honoring Christmas "in his heart" all the year long.

Cars: Right in the midst of his newfound friendship with the townsfolk and possibly love with Miss Sally, Lightning's Third Plot Point is thrust upon him. Doubting the sincerity of Lightning's newfound virtues, Doc has called in the media. Lightning is given the very escape route he's been craving all along. His ability to get to his tie-breaker race in time is practically gift-wrapped for him. But as he is suddenly faced with the realization that the race may mean giving up the peace and happiness he's found in Radiator Springs, Lightning has to be dragged away by Mack.

QUESTIONS TO ASK ABOUT YOUR CHARACTER'S ARC IN THE THIRD PLOT POINT

1. What crushing event and/or revelation turns your character's apparent success into the worst defeat yet?

2. How was this defeat enabled by the character's refusal, thus far, to completely reject his Lie?

3. How does this defeat force your character to face the true ramifications of the Lie?

4. How can this defeat offer the character a clear path toward the Thing He Wants?

5. If he takes this path, how will it force him to reject the Thing He Needs?

6. How can you set up a clear and decided choice between the Thing He Needs and the Thing He Wants?

7. Which will he choose?

8. How can you literally or symbolically represent death in this scene as a way of reinforcing the demise of your character's Lie-empowered old self?

By this point, you should be able to see how the plot points *steer* your story around the corners of your character's arc. The

First Plot Point kicked him out of his Normal World and forced him to start reacting. The Midpoint woke him up out of his reactions and guided him into *taking* action. But that action was, at least partially, just an external response. The character spent the Second Half of the Second Act *acting* in the right way (for the most part), but he hadn't yet quite learned his lesson. Deep down, he still believed he had several options open to him, even though there was only one *right* option within the story.

That, as you've just learned, is why we need the Third Plot Point. The Third Plot Point rips away all those options and forces the character to a place where he has no choice but to be absolutely honest with himself *about* himself and about his situation. In the coming Climax, your protagonist will rise from the ashes, ready to do battle from a place of inner wholeness.

"Life begins at the end of your comfort zone."
—Neale Donald Walsch

12

THE THIRD ACT

CHARACTER ARCS IN the Third Act—the final 25% of the book—are all about intensity. On the story's exterior, the conflict is heating up. The protagonist is a runaway train thundering toward what has now become an inevitable confrontation with the antagonistic force. But, on the inside, he's reeling.

The Third Plot Point sucker-punched him. Something horrible came out of the blue and knocked him woozy. But most important of all: this event revealed his progress in his character arc when he reflexively lashed out and acted according to the *Truth*, instead of his Lie. In doing so, he very well may have shoved the Thing He Wants right out of reach.

He *did* the right thing. And he did it from the depth of his soul. But now he has to live with the consequences. He's grown to believe in the Truth—and yet, the Truth just ruined his life.

On its exterior, the Third Act is all about your character's scrambling to regain his balance before he has to face the antagonist in the Climax. But within your character's interior, the Third Act is all about him figuring out if he *really* wants to serve the Truth after all. Is it worth the price he's just paid? If he's ever going to return to his life of "safety" in the Lie, this is going to be his last chance.

4 Parts of the Character Arc in the Third Act

The landscape of the Third Act offers four important road signs to guide your journey. With the exception of aspects of the first and last of these elements (which need to be placed, respectively, just after the Third Plot Point and just before the Climax), most of these elements will be spread throughout the first half of the Third Act and will be evolved piece by piece, rather than presented in their entirety all at once. As always, pacing—which will be significantly tighter in this section—is the major consideration.

1. Up the Stakes

After his soul-wrenching realization in the Third Plot Point, the character now has to deal with the aftermath. And it's pretty gruesome. He just threw away all his work and all his progress in moving toward the Thing He Wants. Yes, he stood on the moral high ground. Yes, he freed his soul from the oppression of the Lie. But right now, that's not much of a consolation.

The Third Plot Point stuck a knife in the character's back. This is where you give it a little twist. This is the sequel to your Third Plot Point, in which your character reacts to the havoc the Truth just made of his life.

So why not make it even worse? Up the stakes. If the character is emotionally miserable, why not make him physically miserable too?

He just saw his best friend get killed?

Perfect. Now, why not also put him on the run for his life? In a blizzard. With a bullet in his leg.

Don't make it easy for him to come to the conclusion that acting on the Truth was really the best thing he could have done for himself.

Let him wallow in his misery for just a bit. And then have him stand back up. The character must choose between surrendering to his pain and rising to continue the fight. He must realize the price he paid to gain the Thing He Needs was worth the pain.

He raises his chin and faces the wind. He knows he did the right thing—to the point that he'd do it again if he had to. He is now officially remade. That doesn't mean he's not still rough around the edges. He could still topple if somebody punches him hard enough. But from this point on, he *is* a new man.

For Example: In *Green Street Hooligans*, Matt is tremendously uncomfortable with his decision to leave behind the violence of the football firms and abandon his "mates" just as they're headed off to fight the opposing firm that tried to kill his brother-in-law. He knows he's in over his head this time, and he knows he needs to get his sister and nephew to safety, but he can't help feeling like he's walking away when he should be fighting. Still, he gets in the car and starts driving to the airport.

2. Keep the Character Off Balance

In many ways the events at the Third Plot Point are climactic. The character not only acted upon the Truth, he *claimed* it. His arc seems like maybe it's complete. But, in fact, the entire Third Act is about his *continuing* to claim the Truth—not just reflexively, but consciously. His final test won't come until the Climax.

The important distinction here is that the character *has* claimed the Truth, but he still hasn't 100% rejected the Lie. He has already turned the most important corner in his arc—the Truth is rising and the Lie is setting—but the ascendancy of the Truth isn't yet absolute. Even as the character adjusts to his new paradigm, he will continue to experience doubts throughout the Third Act.

These doubts are keeping the character from being either completely fulfilled or completely effective in his new Truth-driven life. He is off-balance and unhappy, still not completely certain he made the right choices earlier. The irony is that, although in choosing the Truth, he has opened the door to happiness and empowerment—he has yet to step through that doorway.

For Example: In *What About Bob?*, Bob agrees it would be best for Leo if Bob went back to New York City. He bravely marches out into the dark forest. But even though he's proven his sanity over and over throughout the second half of the story, he's suddenly riddled with doubts. He surrenders to his fear and runs, screaming, back to the lake house.

3. Prove How Far the Character Has Come

Your character may be currently feeling as if he's making *no* progress, but, of course, that's not true at all. He's made tremendous progress; the person he is now is miles away from the person he was back there at the beginning in the Normal World. You've already dramatically proven this in the Third Plot Point—and will dramatically prove it once again in the Climax. But you should be reinforcing the changes, in smaller ways, throughout the Third Act.

One of the most effective ways to do this is to create an instance in which your character can reject the Lie in a physical way. In the midst of all the other drama and trauma going on, this is usually best presented casually, even offhandedly.

In *The Kid*, the protagonist—who was previously an arrogant jerk—humbly seeks the counsel of a local news anchor, whom he'd memorably snubbed in the First Act. The point of the scene is the counsel itself, not the fact that the protagonist was willing to seek it, and as such it provides a reinforcement of how the character has already changed without making a big deal of it.

For Example: In *Jurassic Park*, Dr. Grant demonstrates his newfound affection for the children when he reassures them before leaving them in (what he believes is) the safety of the main lobby. He pats down Tim's static hair and teases, "Big Tim, the human piece of toast"—something he would never have contemplated in the beginning of the story.

4. Renew the Attack Upon the Character's New Paradigm

Prior to the Climax (which begins roughly halfway through the Third Act—and which we'll discuss in depth in the next chapter), the character's new paradigm of Truth should come under a penultimate assault. In most stories, this renewed attack will be initiated by a character *other* than the main antagonist (who should be saving his big guns for the Climax itself). The attack might come from a minor antagonist, a skeptical or fearful ally, or even the character's own inner doubts.

The point of this attack is to batter the protagonist's doubts about the Truth. The Lie should be reinforced in convincing and attractive terms. If the protagonist would only go back to the Lie, surely he would have a better chance of winning the battle—or maybe even avoiding it altogether. The protagonist shakes his head, rejecting the bad advice, but he *is* tempted. The more convincing the attack and the greater the peril of the protagonist's relapsing, the higher the tension will be.

Sometimes this renewed attack will segue right into the final climactic decision itself. If not, be wary of intensifying the attack too much at this point. The final and most powerful assault should come from the antagonist himself in the midst of the Climax. This renewed attack should logically lead up to the Lie's final attack and the character's final rejection of it. Pay attention to the needs of your story's pacing. Sometimes, the only renewed attack your story will be able to support this close to the Climax is a brief paragraph or two of a minor character's shaking his head and telling the protagonist, "Are you *crazy?*"

For Example: In *Jane Eyre*, just before the Climax (in which she will flee back to Thornfield, fearing for Rochester's life), Jane is subjected to a brutal attack upon her new Truth. Her cousin St. John Rivers insists her new Truth is a selfish and worthless pursuit. He uses her own former beliefs against her to try to convince her she can only live a worthwhile life if she enters a loveless marriage with him and joins him as a missionary in India.

FURTHER EXAMPLES OF THE CHARACTER'S ARC IN THE THIRD ACT

A Christmas Carol: Most of Scrooge's Third Act is a progression of the Third Plot Point scene, in which the terrifyingly silent third spirit shows him the bleak future that awaits him. Although Scrooge is currently in no physical danger, he is shown a future in which he will not only be friendless, but in which he will die. Scrooge has come far since the beginning of the story, but he isn't yet convinced money isn't the ultimate deciding point in a man's worth. The Third Act is all about proving his own worthlessness to the rest of the world, despite his money—as evidenced by his neighbors' heartless response to his death. Scrooge's heartache over Tiny Tim's death and the Cratchits' grief proves his evolution.

Cars: After being dragged away from his friends in Radiator Springs, without even being able to say goodbye, Lightning is an emotional mess. He's about to compete in the race for the Piston Cup—the thing he's been after all movie long—but he can't focus. He's having a hard time even finding a reason to care about this all-important tie-breaking race. His rejection of his "solo mio" attitude is jeopardizing this crucial moment in his career. He doesn't quite understand what's come over him, but he does prove his changed attitude when he humbly thanks Mack for filling in for his fired pit crew. Just as the climactic race begins, antagonist Chick Hicks mocks Lightning for losing his focus and missing his opportunity to "schmooze" the valuable Dinoco sponsor. Lightning is distracted and gets a slow start in the race.

QUESTIONS TO ASK ABOUT YOUR CHARACTER'S ARC IN THE THIRD ACT

1. How does your character react to the Third Plot Point?

2. How has his embrace of the Truth made a mess of his life and, specifically, his pursuit of his plot goal?

3. How can you up the stakes by forcing him into both physical and emotional straits?

4. How do these straits force your character to reconsider whether or not the Truth is the right choice for him?

5. How does he rise from these doubts determined to cling to the Truth?

6. What doubts is the character still experiencing about the Truth?

7. How is his inability to completely reject the Lie keeping him from total happiness and empowerment?

8. How are your character's attitudes and actions different in the Third Act from how they were in the First? How can you subtly reinforce the difference prior to the Climax?

9. How will your character's devotion to the Truth be put to the test? What character or situation will you use to try to tempt or bully your protagonist back into serving the Lie?

The Third Act is where you get to tie off your story's loose ends. When it comes to character arcs, those loose ends include testing the character's devotion to the Truth and showing his final growing pains as he sheds the Lie and moves forward to face his ultimate test in the Climax.

The Third Act should be an exciting and tension-laden section of your story. But it's also an all-business section, as you focus on getting all the pieces—both character and plot—assembled for that final showdown. If you've set up your character's arc correctly in the previous 90% of your story, you'll already have everything in place for an incredible character transformation in the Climax.

"The truth will set you free.
But not until it is finished with you."
—David Foster Wallace

13

THE CLIMAX

I N CHARACTER ARCS, as in plot, the Climax is the dot on the end of the exclamation point. The Climax is the reason for the story. This is where the author reveals what the journey the character just endured was *really* all about—and, in a Positive Change Arc, *why* that journey has turned out to be worth all the heartaches and trauma.

Most important to our discussion, the Climax is where your character proves he really is a changed person. Your readers have witnessed his evolution. They've seen him get shaken up when he was kicked out of his Normal World. They watched his desperate reactions as he tried to regain his footing in the First Half of the Second Act. They saw his revelation at the Midpoint, and his subsequent transition away from his Lie and toward the Truth. They saw him act on the Truth at the Third Plot Point— and pay the price for doing so.

Now, approximately halfway through the Third Act, the conflict has revved to the point where a confrontation *must* happen between the protagonist and the antagonist. If the protagonist is to have any chance of winning that conflict, he must prove he is able to stick with the Truth for the long haul. If he can't gather all the lessons he's learned throughout the story and hang onto them now, when the pressure is greatest, then all will be lost forever.

The Climax is a scene or series of scenes that forces the protagonist to face the main conflict in a decisive confrontation.

The Climax brings the primary conflict to a resolution in a way that fulfills the book's every promise, while still surprising readers in pleasant ways, because not every bit of what happens is what they could have predicted.

The Climax begins near the 90% mark in your story and ends right before the final scene or two.

The Climax will sometimes be divided into two climaxes (the first of which is known as a "faux climax"), depending on how complex the conflict is and how many antagonists the protagonist must confront.

THE CLIMAX

We closed out our discussion of the Third Act by mentioning the renewed attack upon your character's new paradigm (i.e., his embrace of the Truth). Although that renewed attack can take place entirely before the Climax (as it does in *Jane Eyre* when St. John tries to prevent Jane from returning to Thornfield), more often than not, this psychological attack will continue right into the Climax itself. In *The Writer's Journey*, Christopher Vogler explains:

> The psychological meaning of such counterattacks is that neuroses, flaws, habits, desires, or addictions we have challenged may retreat for a time, but can rebound in a last-ditch defense or desperate attack before being vanquished forever.

Timing the Final Rejection of the Lie Your Character Believes

Rejecting the Lie in the Climax

If your exterior conflict with the antagonist is closely related to the protagonist's internal conflict, the protagonist may not throw off this assault until the Climactic Moment itself. The antagonist may batter the protagonist with the Lie, hammering at the newly healed skin that's formed over this old wound. This is the protagonist's weak point, and the antagonist knows it.

Placing the renewed attack and the *final* rejection of the Lie and embrace of the Truth in your Climax allows you to harmonize your exterior and interior conflicts. It also ups the stakes and the tension. Readers sit on the edges of their seats, chewing their nails, because they know full well that if the character can't complete his arc *right now*, the antagonist will destroy him. However, harmonizing the two conflicts also has its downfalls. Because the Climax is such a busy section of your story, you won't always have the time and space to logically complete your character's arc at the same time as he's battling the antagonist. A saber duel to the death isn't usually conducive to involved existential decisions.

Rejecting the Lie Before the Climax

Depending on your story's pacing, you may decide your best choice is to have your character face and defeat his Lie for this final time *before* he charges into the Climax. At this moment, your character will reject the last remnants of doubt about the Lie and step forward to claim the Truth. He is, at last, completely centered—and, as a result, completely empowered to face the antagonist. He is transformed.

The Climax begins as the character acts upon his new Truth, finally and fully. By this point, the character should be finished with all lengthy internal pondering. The uncertainty that remains now is more about the ramifications of his new Truth (will it let him defeat the antagonist? or will it get him killed in the process?) than his own inner choices.

Whatever you decide, keep in mind Jordan McCollum's advice in *Character Arcs*:

> One of the biggest things to watch out for with this type of ending is making sure that the character learns her lesson very close to this climax. If these events occur too far apart, the causal link between learning the lesson and the ultimate success at the climax is weakened. If it's possible to make the final choice in learning the lesson coincide with the climax instead, that helps to prevent the timing problem.

THE CLIMACTIC MOMENT

The Climactic Moment is the climax within the Climax. It's the single moment that resolves the story's overall conflict. In identifying your Climactic Moment, look for (or create) the one scene readers have been waiting for from the beginning of the story. The bad guy dies. The hero proposes. The girl gets the job she's been after.

The conflict ends because the protagonist has finally and conclusively destroyed the antagonistic force. The obstacle between him and his plot goal disappears. This does *not*, however, mean the character necessarily gets the Thing He Wants. Positive Change Arc stories are primarily about the character finding the Thing He Needs.

As such, by the time he reaches his plot goal, the goal itself may have completely transformed, so that he no longer desires the Thing He Wants. (In Clarence Brown's *National Velvet*, Mi Taylor has gained self-respect and no longer wants to steal from the Browns or trade off his father's name.)

Or he may still desire the Thing He Wants, but he rejects it, knowing he can't possess both it and the Thing He Needs. (In *Spider-Man*, Peter Parker rejects the opportunity for a relationship with Mary Jane, because he knows it's the only way to protect her.)

Or his reasons for wanting it may have changed, giving him mixed feelings about his victory. (In *The Kid*, Russ Duritz finally gets rid of his younger self, only to miss having him around.)

Or he may gain the Thing He Wants, but only because he is now focusing on the Thing He Needs. (In Jane Austen's *Emma*, Emma gets to marry Mr. Knightley, but only because she's overcome her selfishness and conceit.)

How Does the Climax Manifest in Character Arcs?

Your character's arc in the Climax could manifest as:

Thor: A renewed attack in which Thor's brother taunts

him, briefly, back into his aggressive mindset. Thor then finally proves his devotion to his new Truth by destroying the Bifrost and (seemingly) any chance of returning to his new love, in order to protect the other realms. The Climactic Moment arrives when Loki (seems to) kill himself, thereby removing himself as the obstacle between Thor and his goal of peace.

Jane Eyre: Jane fully rejects St. John's renewed attack upon her Truth when she hears Rochester calling her. She drops everything to return to him at Thornfield. She proves her new mindset in her determination *not* to marry him—only to be happily surprised when circumstances, including her own transformed self, allow her to be with him after all. The Climactic Moment arrives when she tells Rochester she has returned to him.

Jurassic Park: Dr. Grant battles the raptors at the risk of his own life in order to save the children (not exactly a renewed attack, but it fulfills basically the same function in this action-heavy, character-lite story). The Climactic Moment arrives when the T-Rex crashes into the lobby and destroys the raptors.

Secondhand Lions: Walter holds fast under the physical attack by his mother's abusive boyfriend and refuses to believe his beloved uncles are thieves. He actively claims as Truth their stories of youthful adventure and proves he is willing to be tortured for it. The Climactic Moment arrives later when he confronts his mother and insists she allow him to stay with his uncles.

Toy Story: The other toys scoff at the idea that Woody has changed his tune about Buzz, even after he jumps into the moving van and tries to use RC to save Buzz. The Climactic Moment arrives when he and Buzz land safely in Andy's car.

Three Kings: Archie, Troy, and the Chief's superior officers threaten to court-martial them and return the

Shiite refugees to Saddam's soldiers. The Climactic Moment arrives when, in order to allow everyone to survive, they decide to barter their gold in a deal to get the Shiites across the border to safety.

Green Street Hooligans: The renewed attack comes mostly from within Matt himself. He can't bear the thought of leaving his mates to fight by themselves when he knows they're likely to die. He returns, with his sister and nephew, in an attempt to help them, only to realize the best thing he can do for them is protect his family. The Climactic Moment arrives when his brother-in-law sacrifices his life in order to help them escape.

What About Bob?: The renewed attack comes from Leo, who straps Bob to cases of dynamite, calling it "Death Therapy." After a moment of fear, Bob finally embraces the therapy and is "cured." The Climactic Moment arrives when Bob ends his own ability to torment Leo by accidentally blowing up the lake house and sending Leo into a catatonic state.

FURTHER EXAMPLES OF THE CLIMAX IN CHARACTER ARCS

A Christmas Carol: Scrooge's transformation is basically complete before he exits Christmas Future and enters the Climax. He swears to the Ghost of Christmas Future that he will be a changed man if only he is given the chance to live again. Back in his bedchamber, he immediately sets about proving his change by doing good to everyone he snubbed in the First Act. The Climactic Moment arrives when he decisively demonstrates his devotion to his new Truth of *charity and goodwill* by donating gifts and food to the Cratchits and giving Mr. Cratchit an extravagant raise.

Cars: Lightning embraces his friends and their importance in his life when he joyfully accepts their help as his new pit crew. He races with renewed purpose, making up lost ground. But even though his attitude toward the townsfolk from Radiator Springs is demonstrably different from how he treated them in the beginning, he still hasn't actually *done* anything to prove his devotion to the new Truth. He gets his chance when Chick Hicks acts selfishly (just as Lightning would have at the beginning of the movie) and wrecks the respected old race car The King. Lightning, just about to win the race, sees what's happened and realizes helping The King is more important than winning the race. In a lovely Climactic Moment, he slams on the brakes just before the finish line, allowing Chick to win. He then circles back to help The King finish his race.

QUESTIONS TO ASK ABOUT YOUR CHARACTER'S ARC IN THE CLIMAX

1. How does your character prove he is a changed person in the Climax?

2. Does the renewed attack upon his new Truth happen *before* the Climax or *during* the Climax? What are the pacing challenges of either choice?

3. How does the character's final embrace of the Truth enable his victory in the exterior conflict?

4. Does he fully embrace the Thing He Needs in the Climax?

5. How does he use the Thing He Needs to defeat the antagonist?

6. Does he gain the Thing He Wants?

7. How has his view of the Thing He Wants changed? Does he still want it?

The beginning of your story asked a question: Will the character overcome his Lie to gain the Thing He Needs?

In a Positive Change Arc, the Climax answers that question with a resounding *yes*. More than that, it provides visual and dramatic proof of how the character has been changed by the Truth.

Your character has just completed his arc. He leaves your story a better person than he entered it, and readers can be sure, whatever trials the character may face in the future, he is now better equipped to face them. All that remains is the (very important) emotional mopping up of the Resolution.

"...there are many things that don't really end, anyway, they just begin again in a new way."
—C. JoyBell C.

14

THE RESOLUTION

THE RESOLUTION CAPS character arcs like the cherry on top of a banana split. In some respects, it almost seems to be an extraneous piece of the story. After all, your character's arc is already complete. He irrevocably *proved* his devotion to the Truth in the Climax. He turned his back on the Lie so completely he'll never again be able to surrender to its thrall.

So why do we need the Resolution at all?

This important ending scene(s) is there to bookend the opening scene. In the beginning of your story, you showed your character living in his Normal World, as shaped by the Lie. In the Resolution, you get to show readers the *new* Normal World that has been built by the character's hard-won Truth.

Think of this final scene as a reward. Readers laughed, cried, ached, and triumphed right alongside your character. Don't you think they deserve even just a glimpse of the new and improved life your character is going to live after he rides off into the sunset?

THE RESOLUTION

The Resolution needs to fulfill two primary duties in finishing off your character's arc. The first of those duties is providing an answer to the thematic question that was raised in the story's beginning. The second duty is giving readers a preview of the character's new Lie-free life.

The Thematic Question

In essence, these two duties are two sides of the same coin. Your story's thematic question will have been based upon the character's inner battle between the Lie and the Truth. For example, in *Spider-Man*, the thematic question is famously summed up: Will Peter learn to wield his great power with equally great responsibility?

By the end of the film, that question has been definitively answered by Peter's actions in the Climax. It is then hammered home one final time in the closing scenes, in which we see how he has been so changed by his new Truth that *he is willing to sacrifice the one thing he wants most—the love of Mary Jane Watson—in order to be responsible and protect her.*

Find a way to blatantly state the answer to your story's thematic question—if not through the characters' interactions with each other and the setting, then at least briefly in dialogue. You never want to slap readers in the face with "the moral of the story," but you do want the answer to your thematic question to be perfectly clear.

The Character's New Normal

The Resolution is also the time to back up readers' knowledge with visual proof. Now that the main conflict has been resolved, what will the character do next? How will he act now that he's a changed person?

These changes are often best demonstrated by creating a deliberate contrast between the Normal World in the beginning of the story and the new normal that now exists in the wake of the conflict. Returning the character to the actual physical setting from the beginning of the story, while not absolutely necessary, allows you to dramatically contrast (and therefore highlight) the character's new self with his old world. In *Little Dorrit*, when Amy Dorrit returns to visit the Marshalsea Prison after her father's death in Venice, she is a different person, from top to toe, which is visually obvious in the contrast between the dreary prison and the rich clothing she now wears.

This physical contrast won't work in every story. Sometimes the Normal World from the beginning of the story will have been destroyed, or the character will have no ability or reason to return to it. In these instances, you must prove the difference solely through the character's actions in the Resolution.

In a Positive Change Arc, this final scene should be a fun one—or at least a joyful one. Your character has just been through hell. Hope is rising. The new day is dawning. Play that up for all it's worth.

How Does the Resolution Manifest in Character Arcs?

Your character's arc in the Resolution could manifest as:

Thor: An apology from the previously arrogant Thor to his father, in which he blatantly answers the thematic question: "I have much to learn. I know that now."

Jane Eyre: An epilogue, in which Jane's vastly different new life demonstrates how she is now able to live as Rochester's beloved wife while still maintaining absolute spiritual freedom.

Jurassic Park: A closing scene, in which the previously child-phobic Dr. Grant holds the sleeping children he's come to love, as the helicopter flies them all to safety.

Secondhand Lions: A scene that closely mirrors the opening one, in which a newly empowered Walter marches down the road, greets the dogs and the pig, and tells his uncles they must remain alive long enough to see him through college.

Toy Story: A literal new Normal World (Andy's new home) that acts as the backdrop for a Christmas scene mirroring the early birthday scene that triggered Woody's arc. Here, Woody is happily friends with Buzz, willing to share his top place in Andy's heart.

Three Kings: An ending montage that is both ironic and hopeful, in which the three main characters are shown in their happy post-prison careers—which, it turns out, were funded by just a smidge of that Iraqi bullion after all.

Green Street Hooligans: A final scene, in which Matt, back in the States, proves his new willingness to fight for himself when needed (tempered by his new wisdom about avoiding a fight when possible) by facing down the fellow student who falsely accused him in the beginning—and gaining the proof to clear his name.

What About Bob?: A brilliantly ironic closing scene, in which Bob proves his return to sanity by marrying Leo's sister—which finally brings Leo out of his catatonia.

FURTHER EXAMPLES OF THE RESOLUTION IN CHARACTER ARCS

A Christmas Carol: Dickens ends with a few paragraphs of narrative, spelling out, in no uncertain terms, how Scrooge was changed from that day forward: "…it was always said of him, that he knew how to keep Christmas well, if any man alive possessed the knowledge."

Cars: Lightning backs up his shocking climactic action (in which he sacrificed the Piston Cup in order to help The King finish his last race) by turning down the coveted Dinoco sponsor in order to stand by the Rust-eze sponsors he formerly disdained. He then returns to make Radiator Springs his new training headquarters, breathing new life into his friends' dying town, which also allows him to pursue his dreams without living in the fast lane. He fulfills his promise (and proves he can be trusted) by securing Mater a ride on the Dinoco helicopter, then cements his relationship with Miss Sally. He blatantly offers the answer to his thematic question when he tells The King why he sacrificed the Piston Cup: "This grumpy old race car I know once told me something: It's just an empty cup."

QUESTIONS TO ASK ABOUT YOUR CHARACTER'S ARC IN THE RESOLUTION

1. How does your Resolution contrast your story's beginning?

2. How does your Resolution mirror your story's beginning?

3. How is the character's new Normal World different from the original one?

4. Does the character return to his old Normal World?

5. How does the Resolution answer your story's thematic question?

6. How can you state the answer to the thematic question in dialogue without making it seem like a "moral of the story"?

7. How does your character act differently in the Resolution from how he did at the beginning of the story?

In some ways, learning how to create a solid Positive Change Arc is even more complex than learning how to properly structure a story. If you can understand the psychological workings at the heart of human change, then you'll also understand how to create a story about a character who changes, from worse to better, in a convincing way.

It isn't enough to simply have a character change; he must change in a way that harmonizes with the patterns we all recognize in our own lives and those of our family and friends. Readers will resonate with those patterns in your characters— and they will be moved by them.

PART 2:
THE FLAT ARC

"Better a cruel truth than a comfortable delusion."
—Edward Abbey

15

THE FIRST ACT

NEXT TO THE Positive Change Arc, the Flat Arc is the most popular storyline. Also called the "testing arc," the Flat Arc is about a character who does *not* change. He already has the Truth figured out in the beginning of the story, and he uses that Truth to help him overcome various external tests.

The flat-arc protagonist will be confronted with tremendous opposition. He will at times be shaken. His commitment to the Truth will be tested to the breaking point—but he will never step away from it. He will experience little inner conflict and will not change significantly as a person—although he may sometimes change externally (as per Veronica Sicoe in her blog article "The 3 Types of Character Arc – Change, Growth and Fall"):

> ...the protagonist changes his perspective, learns different skills, or gains a different role. The end-result is not "better" or more than the starting point, just different. The protagonist has not overcome a grand inner resistance or anything, he simply gained a new set of skills or assumed a new position, maybe discovered a talent he forgot he had, or a different vocation.

So how exactly does this work? Why do readers enjoy this self-proclaimed "flat" arc—this story of a static character?

They enjoy it because it is still a story of change. The difference is that the protagonist is the one changing the world *around* him, rather than the world changing the character, as we find in Change Arcs.

By this point, you're already familiar with the foundational principles of the Positive Change Arc. Most of those principles remain true for the Flat Arc, but with some significant variations. In the next three chapters, we're going to be taking a look at how Flat Arcs differ from Positive Change Arcs—and how you can use them to create an awesome story.

THE TRUTH THE CHARACTER BELIEVES

The Positive Change Arc is all about the Lie the Character Believes—which he will spend the entire story overcoming. The Flat Arc, however, is about the *Truth* the Character Believes. In a Flat Arc, the protagonist already has a handle on the Truth, and he will use that Truth to overcome the challenges of the plot—and, probably, to transform a Lie-burdened world.

Your character may very well have a Ghost (which can be used to create interesting depth in his backstory and plausibility for his motivations), but, unlike in a Positive Change Arc, he has already come to peace with it. A Flat Arc will never be a story about a character's search for closure.

This is why we often see Positive Change Arcs in the first book in a series and Flat Arcs in the following books. Marvel's *Thor* movies are a great example. Thor overcomes his Lie in the first movie, so that by the time his second round of adventures arrives, he can use his new Truth to transform the world(s) around him.

THE NORMAL WORLD

In a Flat Arc, the Normal World can manifest in two ways, the first of which is as a good place that represents the character's Truth. In this instance, the Normal World will either be destroyed at the First Plot Point, or, more likely, the character will be forced to journey away from it in order to protect it.

The second possible manifestation of the Normal World is

as a less-than-satisfactory place, which has been cursed by a great Lie—against which the protagonist's Truth will stand in direct opposition. The protagonist will use his Truth to destroy this evil world and build a better one in its place.

Just as in the Positive Change Arc, the Normal World in which the story opens will be a symbol, either of what the protagonist is fighting to protect or what he's fighting to overcome. It sets the stage for the story to follow.

THE CHARACTERISTIC MOMENT

The Characteristic Moment functions almost identically in all three types of arc. The only major difference in the Flat Arc is that the Characteristic Moment must be used to introduce your character's Truth instead of his Lie.

Ask yourself: what skills and beliefs does he possess in the beginning of the story that make him ideally suited to take on the Lie, as represented by the antagonistic force? Come up with an opening scene that illustrates these qualities in an intriguing and sympathetic way.

THE FIRST ACT

Within the first quarter of a Flat-Arc story, your primary responsibilities are going to be setting the stage for the coming conflict. You must introduce the important characters and their respective alignments with either the Truth or the Lie. Just as in a Positive Change Arc, this is the time to lavish some extra attention on the Lie, because within the Lie is always where we discover what is at stake for the protagonist. What horrible things will happen to him and his world if the Lie isn't overthrown?

The character probably won't start out the story with a knowledge of the Lie. He knows the *Truth*, but he may not yet have been confronted with the fact that the Lie is deeply rooted in the world around him. Most of the First Act will be spent with his growing realization that there's something pretty stinky going on in Denmark.

The protagonist may oppose the Lie from the beginning, but he won't confront it head on in the First Act. Sometimes he may even spend the First Act actively *avoiding* a confrontation. He's content in his own mastery of the Truth, and he may not see any need to try to use that Truth to protect or heal the broken world around him. He won't become fully engaged in a battle against the antagonistic force's Lie until the First Plot Point at the end of the First Act.

How Does the First Act Manifest in a Flat Arc?

In the First Act, your Flat Arc could manifest as:

The Hunger Games: A belief that *society should be based on trust and compassion, rather than fear and sadism* (the Truth in opposition to the Lie). Katniss Everdeen lives in a stark Normal World where she remains in constant fear of the government as she struggles to feed and protect her mother and sister. From the first line on, she is shown relentlessly sacrificing for those she cares about (Characteristic Moment), which then escalates dramatically at the Inciting Event, when she takes her sister's place in the reaping. Via elaborations of the Hunger Games, the First Act hammers home the despicability of the Lie-ridden world in which Katniss lives.

Chicken Run: A belief that *it would be better to die trying to escape rather than live in captivity* (the Truth in opposition to the Lie). Ginger the chicken's Normal World is a stalag-like chicken farm run by the villainous Mrs. Tweedy, who stymies Ginger's every attempt to get herself and her friends to safety. The opening montage presents Characteristic Moment after Characteristic Moment, in which Ginger proves her cleverness and tenacity in trying to escape over and over again. The First Act demonstrates the general awfulness of constantly living one step away from the chop (especially when Mrs. Tweedy decides to buy a machine that will turn them all into meat pies), as well as Ginger's absolute devotion to her Truth.

The Last of the Mohicans: A belief that *fighting to protect family is more important than fighting for a perfidious king* (the Truth in opposition to the Lie). Nathaniel's Normal World of beautiful nature and simple but rewarding lifestyles is one worth protecting, but it is threatened by the encroaching war between the French and English and the English Army's determination to force the colonial militia into a battle far from their endangered families. The opening deer hunt proves Nathaniel's absolute sense of belonging within his naturalistic world (Characteristic Moment), and the First Act increasingly pits the peaceful world of his Truth against the threat of the war's Lie.

Gladiator: A belief that *Rome must continue to be a light in the darkness of a barbaric world, rather than the slave of a single man* (the Truth in opposition to the Lie). Maximus's Normal World has been that of Rome, as ruled by the wise and benevolent Marcus Aurelius, but it's already beginning to crumble: Aurelius is dying, and his unstable son waits in the wings. Throughout the First Act, Maximus is faced with the choice of returning home to his family or remaining to protect Rome. (This is a good example of an instance in a Flat Arc, in which the Thing the Character Wants and the Thing the Character Needs actually stand in conflict, just as in a Positive Change Arc—if only briefly.)

Sense & Sensibility: A belief that *a sensible approach to life and love will bear greater fruits than will wild emotional abandon* (the Truth in opposition to the Lie). Elinor Dashwood, as the only person of strong logic left in her family, lives in a Normal World that is under constant assault from her mother's and sisters' emotional needs—everything from her mother's desire for a nicer house than they can afford to Marianne's romantic passions. Elinor is introduced as the "eldest daughter, whose advice was so effectual, [and who] possessed a strength of understanding, and coolness of judgment…" (Characteristic Moment). Elinor spends the First Act trying to manage her mother's tangled affairs and her sisters' heated emotions.

Captain America: The Winter Soldier: A belief that *freedom can't be achieved by a police state monitoring and destroying threats before they happen* (the Truth in opposition to the Lie). Steve Rogers's current Normal World is a shaky one, in which he is increasingly uncomfortable with the jobs SHIELD is asking him to do, supposedly in the name of freedom. Almost right away, he is shown distrusting the motives of those who are using him as a weapon to achieve their own ends (Characteristic Moment). After he learns what Director Fury has up his sleeve, he knows he can't maintain his Truth if he remains in SHIELD, and he spends the bulk of the First Act contemplating simply walking away.

True Grit: A belief that *justice is worth pursuing and even sacrificing for, and that a careless attitude about social justice can only create anarchy* (the Truth in opposition to the Lie). Mattie Ross's belief in this Truth is challenged throughout by murderers, thieves, well-meaning townsfolk, and even her own lawmen allies. She lives in a stark, cruel frontier, in which justice is too often sacrificed or compromised for convenience's sake (Normal World). The world in which she lives is gray; Mattie, in contrast, is as black and white as they come. From the very beginning, she sets out with the goal of bringing her father's murderer to justice (Characteristic Moment), and when, throughout the First Act, she finds the institutions of justice opposing or hindering her progress, she becomes increasingly determined to circumvent them altogether and get the job done herself.

Batman Begins: A belief (thanks to the flashback sequences in the First Act, in which Bruce Wayne undergoes a miniature Positive Change Arc) that *"justice is about harmony.*

Revenge is about you making yourself feel better" (the Truth in opposition to the Lie). Within the "real-time" chronology of the First Act, Bruce is already committed to this Truth: he just needs to be shown a way to implement it. His Normal World is a glittering façade of wealth that hides the rotten epicenter of Gotham's corruption. After being rescued by Ducard in the opening sequence, he spends the First Act equipping himself to fight that corruption—only to learn the true depth of the stakes when it turns out the Lie has infiltrated even the supposedly righteous League of Shadows.

QUESTIONS TO ASK ABOUT THE FIRST ACT IN A FLAT ARC

1. What Truth does your character already believe at the beginning of your story?

2. Does he have a Ghost in his backstory that prompted this belief?

3. What Lie, as represented by the antagonistic force, will he have to fight?

4. Does his Normal World represent the Truth he will be fighting to protect—or does it represent the Lie he must overthrow in order to establish the Truth?

5. If the former, how can you illustrate the encroaching threat of the Lie upon that Normal World?

6. When will your protagonist first become aware of the threat of the Lie?

7. Is the protagonist initially reluctant to engage in a battle with the Lie?

8. If he is already committed to battling the Lie, what obstacles in the First Act prevent him from a full-on confrontation with the Lie?

9. What Characteristic Moment can you use to illustrate your character's devotion to the Truth—and the resultant knowledge and skills he is able to wield?

10. How can your opening illustrate the Lie that opposes the protagonist?

11. Throughout the First Act, how can you use the Lie to prove what is at stake for the protagonist?

A Flat Arc offers the opportunity for you to create a competent, committed protagonist who can transform the world around him. Many heroic stories feature Flat Arcs, not because they're plot-heavy, but because Flat Arcs allow for explosive change within the world around the character. Don't make the mistake of thinking Flat Arcs are less complicated or significant than Positive Change Arcs. They're every bit as exciting and powerful in their own right.

"In a time of deceit
telling the truth
is a revolutionary act."
—George Orwell

16

THE SECOND ACT

THE SECOND ACT is the beating heart of your story—and that's just as true in a Flat Arc as it is in a Change Arc. The Second Act is all about releasing the protagonist upon an unsettled world. At first, he is forced to react to the major event at the First Plot Point and grapple with the Lie. Then everything changes at the Midpoint, when new knowledge about himself and/or the world allows him to start taking action by going on the offensive.

In comparison to a Positive Change Arc, the difference in a Flat Arc's Second Act is that the emphasis is not on the protagonist's discovering and confronting his own inner misconceptions. Rather, the Second Act in a Flat Arc is where he will be discovering the Lie embedded in the world around him. He will have to figure out, first, whether or not he *wants* to take on that Lie, and, second, how he can best use his Truth to obtain his goal, triumph over the antagonistic force, and uproot the Lie from the lives of those around him.

Your character may already wield the Truth, but the Second Act will see him placed under siege by the Lie. He will have every reason to take the easy way out and surrender his Truth to that Lie, or perhaps even just pack up his Truth and walk away from the Lie without ever trying to confront it. In short, just because your character's arc is flat doesn't mean it's going to be easy.

THE FIRST PLOT POINT

This major scene is the first turning point in your story. It marks the end of the First Act and the beginning of the Second. It's that first "doorway," through which your character must walk. He will leave the Normal World of the First Act and irrevocably enter the new "adventure" world of the story.

The First Plot Point functions very similarly in both change and Flat Arcs. It will be a major (probably catastrophic) event that will upend your character's world and force him into a reaction that will pit his personal Truth directly against the world's Lie.

Up to this point, he will have been seeking to avoid a confrontation. Maybe he just plain doesn't want to deal with the conflict. The world's going to hell in a handbasket, but it's not his fight. Or it could be that he spent the First Act *wanting* to overcome the Lie, but hoping it could be done diplomatically and peacefully, without a head-on confrontation. In either case, the First Plot Point will be a shocking event that suddenly makes the world's external problems very personal to the protagonist.

THE FIRST HALF OF THE SECOND ACT

After the world-rocking events of the First Plot Point, the protagonist must choose to actively engage the Lie. He knows he already possesses the necessary weapon—the Truth—and he now realizes he has a responsibility to wield it. His direct plot goal may not be "overcome the Lie," but whatever he's after will require the destruction of the Lie if he's going to obtain it.

In the First Half of the Second Act, your protagonist is still going to be in reaction mode. This does not mean he's passive; it just means he's not in control of the conflict—the antagonistic force is. Usually, the reason the character is not in control is because he lacks important information. By this point, he obviously knows there's a major problem in the world around him, and he knows he has to do something to overcome it. But he probably doesn't yet know the extent of that problem. He doesn't yet know how deep the Lie's rabbit hole goes.

In contrast to the Positive Change Arc, the character is going to spend the First Half of the Second Act getting punished for believing the Truth. Everyone around him will try to convince him he's an idiot for opposing the Lie. His devotion to the Truth is going to be tested, and for these tests to have any teeth, the character *must* become less than certain about the Truth. He needs to seriously consider whether he's actually following the Truth after all. Could it be that he's wrong and everyone else is right? Maybe the Truth is really a Lie, and the Lie is really the Truth! For anywhere from a few moments to a few scenes, he's not quite certain what to believe. But he never fully turns his back on the Truth.

THE MIDPOINT

The Midpoint is your story's centerpiece. It's a reversal caused by an important revelation. Something happens that provides the protagonist with new information. Suddenly, all the questions from the first half begin to find answers. He figures out what the antagonistic force is *really* up to and/or capable of, and he sees for the first time how corrupted and powerful the Lie really is.

This is all going to seem a little depressing on the surface, since the protagonist's Truth suddenly appears a tiny weapon in comparison to that huge Lie he's trying to fight. But the hero isn't depressed (well, maybe for a minute or two). Rather, he's suddenly afire with new determination. Now everything makes sense. His doubt about whether or not he's following the right course dissipates, and he becomes 100% committed to doing whatever he must to triumph over the Lie.

Just as in the Positive Change Arc, the Midpoint and its revelations must include a Moment of Truth. The difference here is that this redemptive moment of insight and new resolve

168 | K.M. WEILAND

isn't offered *to* the protagonist. Instead, the protagonist is the one who (figuratively or literally) offers the Truth to the world around him. Allies who previously resisted the Truth (and who will be, essentially, following Positive Change Arcs of their own) will begin to see the light. Enemies (who are following Negative Change Arcs) will scoff and toss the Truth's offered grace right back into the protagonist's face.

THE SECOND HALF OF THE SECOND ACT

The Midpoint has changed everything for the protagonist. His doubts have been, for the most part, swept aside. He knows what he's up against, and he knows what he has to do to confront the Lie. It's a long shot, of course (after all, all good stories are, essentially, underdog stories), but he's willing to die trying if he has to.

If the First Half of the Second Act is about the protagonist's reacting, the Second Half is about his taking action. My editor Cathi-Lyn Dyck comments:

> The types of actions or non-actions the character takes will be directly related to which act of the story she's in. In Act 1, her reactions and decisions will be based on normal life as she's known it till now. [In] Act 2a, individual reactions and decisions arise from her ongoing reaction to the first plot point. [In] Act 2b, they arise from how the midpoint revelation changes her perspective. And [in] Act 3, [they arise] from the intention to finally resolve the [dramatic question].

Now that the protagonist has seen the true power of the Lie, he's also seen its weakness (even if it's just a tiny one), and he's determined to exploit it. His aggressive actions in this section will dramatically affect the world around him. Even as the Lie bears down hard, the world is beginning to awaken to the true horror of the belief they've been cultivating all story long. They're starting to rally to the protagonist's cause, and the antagonistic force is starting to sweat. The Second Act will end with what seems to be a definitive victory on the protagonist's part—but it's really just a setup for what will be his greatest defeat yet at the Third Plot Point.

How Does the Second Act Manifest in a Flat Arc?

In the Second Act, your Flat Arc could manifest as it does in the following examples:

The Hunger Games: When the First Plot Point plants Katniss squarely in enemy territory—Capitol City—she is hurtled, against her will, into the world of the Lie. She doesn't care so much about defeating the Lie. She just cares about surviving, even if it means taking out fellow tribute Peeta. What she doesn't yet fully comprehend is that, in order to survive, she's going to have to take down the world of the Lie first. She only begins to fully realize this at the Midpoint, when Peeta saves her after the tracker jacker attack, and she puts aside even the possibility of playing President Snow's game: she won't kill Peeta. The world reflects this back to her when the Gamemaker announces that two tributes from the same district can share the victory. She finds a wounded Peeta and starts making plans to save both their lives.

Chicken Run: Ginger discovers an opportunity for escape when circus performer Rocky crash lands inside the pen. She coerces him into supposedly helping her teach the other chickens how to fly, even though no one else understands the necessity of escaping. At the Midpoint, Ginger realizes Mrs. Tweedy is going to kill them all and finally convinces the others that if they don't "escape or die trying," they're all going to die anyway. Rocky (who is a Positive Change Arc character) makes the most prominent shift away from the Lie and begins seriously trying to help Ginger and the others.

The Last of the Mohicans: Nathaniel's Normal World collides with the world of the Lie when he rescues Cora and Alice Munro from Magua's ambush. He has no desire to try to use his Truth to change the exterior world of the British Army, but then he discovers his friends have been murdered by Indians allied with the French. He commits to returning the sisters to their soldier father at Ft. William Henry, in order to warn the other colonists fighting with the British. After Nathaniel helps the colonists desert back to their families, the antagonist shows the true depth of the Lie by arresting him at the Midpoint. As a result, the world around Nathaniel begins to shift toward the Truth—as is most evident in Cora's changed mindset, but also, more subtly, in Duncan's.

Gladiator: After Maximus refuses to join hands with the patricide Commodus, his wife and son are murdered in a shocking First Plot Point, and Maximus himself is enslaved as a gladiator. He stumbles through the First Half of the Second Act, apathetic to life. Even though he is disgusted by the blood he is forced to spill for the sake of entertainment, he goes through a period in which he struggles to find the strength and conviction to fight for his Truth. Everything changes at the Midpoint when he is sent to fight in Rome and is able to tell Commodus, to his face, that he won't rest until he can remove him from his father's throne. His motives are further cleared up and brought back into alignment with the Truth when he agrees to help Lucilla take down Commodus—not for the sake of vengeance, but for Rome's peace and security. Throughout the Second Half of the Second Act, he victoriously battles his way through Commodus's desperate attempts to kill him. With every victory, he rallies the people nearer to his cause.

Sense & Sensibility: After Elinor and her family end up in a tiny Devonshire cottage, and Marianne meets both her would-be suitors—the upright Colonel Brandon and the passionate Willoughby—Elinor spends most of the First Half of the Second Act struggling to help her emotional family cope. Her sensible approach is brought under siege when the man she loves refuses to ask for her hand, even after dropping in for a strange visit. The Midpoint throws her world topsy-turvy and cements the importance of her Truth when Willoughby abruptly dumps a hysterical Marianne and leaves the neighborhood without explanation. Even amidst her own heartbreak, Elinor steadily guides her family through the tempest of the Second Half of the Second Act.

Captain America: The Winter Soldier: Steve's indecision about his loyalty to SHIELD ends once and for all when Nick Fury is shot by his own people. From that moment on, Steve is committed to following his own principles and figuring out what's really going on at SHIELD—especially after SHIELD tries to kill him and then brands him a fugitive. He goes on the run and chases the Lie to its rabbit hole. This is where, at the Midpoint, he finally realizes the full extent of SHIELD's corruption and their plan to kill millions of people "in the name of freedom." At that point, he has everything to lose and little chance of winning, but his outlook brightens because "I just like to know who I'm fighting." His Truth's effect on the Lie is particularly evident in Black Widow's change of attitude toward both him and SHIELD in the Second Half of the Second Act.

True Grit: Mattie takes the Lie-ridden world by storm when she hires Rooster Cogburn—the "meanest" marshal—to help her go after her father's murderer Tom Chaney. In this instance, Mattie's strong Truth-driven decision is actually more dramatic than the preceding challenge to her Truth: the law establishment's refusal to do anything about her father's murder. Mattie is an especially strong catalyst character, who personally drives practically every major moment in the story. She spends the First Half of the Second Act bearing up under Rooster's and the Texas Ranger LaBoeuf's alternately self-centered and well-meaning attempts to sway her from her mission. At the Midpoint, she doggedly accompanies the men into the Indian Nation, despite their insistence that she remain behind. Her determination forces them into a Moment of Truth where they recognize the resilience of her Truth and reluctantly welcome her as an ally. The conflict in the Second Half of the Second Act is primarily external, as they track down the outlaw gang with whom Chaney is running. The character arc plays out steadily, as Mattie slowly but surely bends the lawmen into a better understanding of both her and her Truth.

Batman Begins: After fully committing himself to his new role by literally burning his bridges behind him, Bruce returns to Gotham. Most of the First Half of the Second Act revolves around his external activities in preparing his Batman persona and researching crime lord Carmine Falcone's plans. His Truth is tested by pretty much everyone—via Alfred's concerns, Rachel's doubt, and even Gordon's initial skepticism. At the Midpoint, he crashes into the heart of the drug operation Falcone is running under Dr. Crane's direction and dramatically reveals his "sign" to the city. From here on out, he's not only committed to the Truth, he *is*, in essence, *the Truth*. Gordon rallies to his cause, and the city—including Rachel—begins to believe he's capable of taking down the Lie. He still faces opposition, most notably when Alfred warns him he's in danger of megalomania if he gets "lost inside this monster of yours." This is a great example of how a well-played Flat Arc keeps readers on their toes: they're never 100% sure the protagonist *is* right. Even the protagonist himself isn't 100% sure. Maybe he's headed down the wrong path. Maybe his Truth isn't so true. Maybe he's veering *away* from the Truth without knowing it. But, just as the protagonist should in a true Flat Arc, Bruce manages to continue walking the tightrope of his Truth, if only just barely.

QUESTIONS TO ASK ABOUT THE SECOND ACT IN A FLAT ARC

1. How does the First Plot Point force your character into a direct confrontation with the Lie?

2. Does he willingly confront the Lie—or does he confront it only because he has no other choice?

3. How will the character be tempted away from his Truth?

4. How close will he come to actually abandoning the Truth and embracing the Lie?

5. What allies will initially resist his devotion to the Truth?

6. How will those allies eventually be changed by the Truth?

7. How will his enemies resist his Truth?

8. How will those enemies become even more entrenched in the Lie as a result?

9. Is the character's main plot goal directly related to defeating the Lie in the world around him?

10. If not, why will he have to overcome the Lie in order to reach his main plot goal?

11. What doesn't the character understand about the Lie in the first half of the story?

12. What important information will he learn about the Lie and the antagonistic force at the Midpoint?

13. How can he offer a Moment of Truth either generally to the world around him or specifically to his allies and/ or the antagonist?

14. At the Midpoint, what weakness does the protagonist find in the Lie that he can exploit in the second half?

The reason many Flat Arcs are perceived as "plot-heavy" is that their emphasis is upon the changes in the world around the protagonist. But it is the *protagonist*'s actions in support of his Truth that cause those changes. More importantly, his Truth-driven actions in the Second Act will begin to change the supporting characters. Thanks to his Flat Arc, they will be following Positive or Negative Change Arcs of their own.

"The truth does not change
according to our ability to stomach it."
—Flannery O'Connor

17

THE THIRD ACT

THE THIRD ACT is where we find arguably the greatest similarities between the Flat Arc and the Positive Change Arc, since in both types of story the protagonist will have a full grasp on the Truth by this point. The primary difference, of course, is that the protagonist in a Flat Arc will have already been in possession of that Truth almost universally *throughout* the story.

The other difference is that, in a Flat Arc, select supporting characters (who are representatives of the world around the protagonist) will have reached the point in their Change Arcs where the protagonist's Truth will have convinced them to reject the Lie. The protagonist will still be facing overwhelming odds, but he won't be facing them alone. Even should he die now, his cause will continue thanks to the converts he's made along the way.

This does not *necessarily* mean all Flat Arcs will demonstrate deep themes. Every Flat Arc will present a protagonist whose views are opposed to the antagonist-influenced world. But those views may not be deep moral issues. Sometimes the Truth can be as simple as the evergreen "the bad guy will destroy the world if he isn't stopped." Flat Arcs of this type are popular in action stories, and while their thematic elements aren't as obvious, they're still viable story forms.

THE THIRD PLOT POINT

After what seemed to be a great victory at the end of the Second Act, the tables will be completely turned on your protagonist, and he'll be smacked back down into his most intense defeat yet. No matter what kind of arc your character is pursuing, the Third Plot Point is going to be his low moment—his breaking point. He's going to face down death, figuratively or literally, and he's going to come to terms with his fears, re-embrace the Truth, and rise with renewed determination and vigor.

In a Flat Arc, the protagonist won't actually doubt the Truth, but he *will* be brought to a point where he seriously doubts his *ability* to use the Truth to defeat the Lie. This is the scene where he throws stuff against the wall and rages against his own impotence. What's the point of the fight—what's the point of everything he's already suffered—if all he's been able to do so far is put a *dent* in the antagonistic force's armor?

Make the Third Plot Point as personal as possible for your protagonist. The antagonistic force needs to hit him where it hurts. This isn't just a defeat. This is a battle that kills his best friend, threatens his wife and children, or perhaps even ends with him wounded and in captivity. Everything seems lost.

THE THIRD ACT

The first half of the Third Act will be all about the protagonist's reacting to the Third Plot Point. By now, supporting characters will have learned to embrace the Truth, thanks to the protagonist's influence. Often, this will be a segment in which these characters will comfort and encourage the protagonist, reminding him how much he's already accomplished in helping *them* see past the Lie. Or the protagonist may see supporting characters staggering under their own doubts, and he will pick himself back up in order to strengthen them once more.

He will have to gather his remaining resources and personnel and figure out what to do next. Even though the protagonist possesses the ultimate weapon of the Truth, the Third Plot

Point has left him at a serious disadvantage. He will have only one chance left to hit the antagonistic force—and it's a long shot at best.

The undercurrent will be all about your protagonist's re-pledging himself to the Truth. By this point, he is committed up to his neck. He will do anything to accomplish his goal—even if it means sacrificing his life. Since this segment will be a comparatively quiet and thoughtful sequel to the Third Plot Point, it provides a good opportunity to have the protagonist outright discuss the Truth and the Lie, and why he has chosen (and re-chosen) to be so committed to it.

THE CLIMAX

The Climax begins roughly halfway through the Third Act (around the 90% mark). This is where your protagonist puts into play his final assault against the antagonistic force and the Lie. Just as in a Positive Change Arc, the protagonist's Truth will be directly pitted against the antagonistic force's Lie. These two intangibles will be far more important in deciding the battle than will any display of physical power.

The difference between the Climax in a Positive Change Arc and the Climax in a Flat Arc is that the Flat-Arc protagonist is already completely solid in his own belief of the Truth. The antagonistic force will fling the Lie in the character's face and try to get him to weaken, but the protagonist won't budge. Even if the antagonist gets the upper hand physically, he will discover his own ineffectiveness in the face of the protagonist's resolve.

Supporting characters who are following Change Arcs may reach a climactic moment when their devotion to the Truth is tested one last time, but the prominence you give these moments will depend on the characters' importance to the story. The protagonist always needs to be the primary catalyst in the final victory. If a supporting character's final declaration of the Truth is the key to winning the conflict, then he becomes, in essence, the primary character. This isn't necessarily a problem if you have a Flat Arc character and a Positive Change Arc character sharing the lead. But never lose track of which arc needs to be kept at the forefront of the story.

THE RESOLUTION

As in any type of story, the Resolution exists to prove how the conflict has changed either the characters or the world. In a Flat Arc, the changes will be most evident in the supporting cast and the world around the protagonist. The Truth will now be ascendant over the Lie. Supporting characters who were changed by Truth will need to be presented in closing characteristic moments that prove the new direction their lives are now about to take. Supporting characters who believed the Truth all along will now be free to embrace and practice it.

If the Normal World in the story's beginning was evil and Lie-ridden, it will now have been destroyed, and the protagonist and his supporters will be able to build a better world on top of the rubble. If the Normal World was based on the Truth in the first place, the characters will now be able to return to it and live in peace.

The protagonist himself won't have changed dramatically. But that doesn't mean certain aspects of his persona and lifestyle may not be different. He may decide to hang up his gun and become a farmer, now that there's no longer a threat to his Truth. Or he may have gained significant new skills along the way that now allow him to pursue a different life. Or he may travel on to fight the Lie in a different place. In fact, just about everything about your protagonist *could* be different at the end of the story. But the one thing that must remain the same is his absolute devotion to the story's core Truth.

HOW DOES THE THIRD ACT MANIFEST IN A FLAT ARC?

In the Third Act, your Flat Arc could manifest as it does in the following examples:

The Hunger Games: After the seeming victory in which Katniss learns how to obtain the medicine she needs to save Peeta's life, she risks everything in a showdown at the Cornucopia. She makes it back to the cave, heals Peeta, and collapses into delirium from her own injuries. This is a comparatively weak Third Plot Point, since the true emotional low point came earlier when Katniss's young ally Rue was murdered. Here, the emphasis is on Katniss's growing affection for Peeta and her determination to get them both out of the games alive. They battle together—symbolically reinforcing their own Truth—to conquer the last of the rival tributes, only to have the Lie hit them with all its power when President Snow tries to force them to kill each other. Katniss never wavers from her Truth and uses it to outsmart the Gamemaker and get both herself and Peeta declared co-victors. The Resolution hints at the changes her actions have wrought in the world around them.

Chicken Run: After a round of seeming successes (Rocky's rescuing Ginger, the pie machine's blowing up, Rocky and Ginger's recognizing their feelings for one another, and Ginger's belief that Rocky will fly for them now that his wing is healed), the Third Plot Point hits Ginger hard when Rocky abandons them and she realizes he lied about being able to fly. After a moment of bitter defeat, she rallies herself and the others with the new plan to build a plane. At the Climax, they're forced to launch the plane early, and thanks to a changed Rocky's return, they manage to pull it off. But the final defeat of Mrs. Tweedy's attempt to reinforce the Lie belongs to Ginger. In the Resolution, the chickens literally arrive in a new world—one full of green grass and without fences.

The Last of the Mohicans: After just barely managing to escape the massacre incited by the vengeful Magua, Nathaniel is forced to abandon Cora, Alice, and Duncan in order to escape being captured by the Indians. Nathaniel's absolute devotion to his Truth (*protecting those he loves*) never wavers. He swears to Cora that he will find her and rescue her, no matter how long it takes. And, as it turns out, it doesn't take that long. He manages—with help from a changed Duncan—to secure her freedom, but not Alice's. The Climax actually shifts attention away from Nathaniel and onto his adopted brother Uncas, as he sacrifices his life in an attempt to save Alice, but the thrust of the Truth remains the same. In the Resolution, they return to Nathaniel's peaceful world—free from Magua's and Col. Munro's Lie—in which Nathaniel and Cora must start anew together.

Gladiator: Maximus and Lucilla rally senators and soldiers to their secret plan to overthrow Commodus. But they are discovered, and several key members of the plot, including Maximus's loyal servant (making the defeat even more personal to Maximus), are murdered. Maximus is captured and stabbed by Commodus. In the Climax, Commodus battles the wounded Maximus, one on one, in the Coliseum, and Maximus rallies to defeat the evil emperor—only to finally succumb to his own mortal wounds. He leaves behind him a Rome that is a better place, even for the gladiators. As Juba says in the final line, "Now we are free."

Sense & Sensibility: On the heels of learning the truth about Willoughby's abandonment of Marianne, Elinor's own romantic hopes are finally and completely slain when her own love Edward Ferrars is forced to announce his engagement to the horrible Lucy Steele. Even Elinor's pragmatism crumbles for a moment as she allows herself to break down in sorrow. But she gathers herself back together and turns her attention to getting Marianne back home. Tragedy strikes and the Climax begins when Marianne runs off in the rain and becomes dangerously ill. In the end, Elinor's patience and good sense are rewarded when Lucy jilts Edward, freeing him to finally seek and receive Elinor's hand. The Resolution finds both Elinor and her newly sensible sister Marianne wedded blissfully to Edward and Colonel Brandon, respectively.

Captain America: The Winter Soldier: The Third Plot Point finds Steve and his allies captured and headed for execution. Even worse (and more personal), Steve has just been sucker-punched with the realization that the enemy he's been fighting all along is really his long-lost best friend. He still wholeheartedly believes in the Truth that he must destroy SHIELD, but now that mission is going to come at a higher price than even he imagined. He moves forward, with the encouragement of his allies, and unflinchingly puts the Truth before his own feelings and even his own life. In the end, his actions create a new world, free of SHIELD, in which everyone must scramble to readjust their mindsets and their lives.

True Grit: Mattie accomplishes a resounding personal victory when she discovers the murderer Tom Chaney watering horses and manages to get the drop on him with her father's huge old revolver. Her confidence in her Truth leads her to believe she can place Chaney under arrest all by herself. And she almost pulls it off—except her revolver misfires and a wounded Chaney takes her prisoner before Rooster and LaBoeuf can intervene. Her emotional low moment arrives when it appears Rooster is willing to abandon her to the outlaw gang. But she rallies and begins exerting her will on gang leader Ned Pepper, who leaves her with Chaney but insists Chaney not harm her. Rooster ends up killing Chaney and rescuing Mattie after she's bitten by a rattlesnake, which relegates her to a comparatively minor role in the Climax. But the force of her personality makes the scenario work, since everything Rooster does is ultimately either because of the changes she has worked on him throughout the story or because of her own dynamism acting directly through him in the Climax itself. In the end,

Mattie herself is physically changed by the loss of her arm, but her mindset remains solid (even rigid). Rooster and LaBoeuf are changed more subtextually—especially Rooster in his affection for Mattie—than dramatically. But, as the epilogue shows, the world around Mattie changes markedly in subsequent years, thanks to the actions of many law-abiding western citizens, all of whom are represented in the story by Mattie herself.

Batman Begins: R'as Al Ghul hits Bruce Wayne where it hurts when he arrives to personally destroy Gotham—starting with Bruce and his family's manor. Bruce is wounded and barely escapes being trapped in the burning house. He surveys the ruin and expresses his absolute doubt—not in his devotion to his Truth but in his ability to actually do anything to further it. He says, "What have I done, Alfred? Everything my family… everything my father and his father built…" Alfred, who has previously expressed doubts about Bruce's mission, now encourages him and urges him to pick himself up and try again. Renewed, Bruce flings himself into the chaos R'as Al Ghul has unleashed in Gotham. Practically alone in the battle, he faces R'as and uses his Truth to finally defeat him. In the Resolution, Gordon clearly describes the new world Bruce has created. He says, "You really started something—bent cops running scared, hope on the streets." The new world isn't perfect, since the story will continue in sequels, but the movie makes it clear Gotham City has been definitively changed by Bruce Wayne's beliefs and actions.

QUESTIONS TO ASK ABOUT THE THIRD ACT IN A FLAT ARC

1. How is the Truth now evident in the lives of the previously Lie-driven supporting characters?

2. What defeat will nearly break your protagonist—physically, emotionally, or both—at the Third Plot Point?

3. How can he face death—literally or figuratively—in the Third Plot Point?

4. How can you make this defeat as personal as possible for the protagonist?

5. How will your protagonist doubt his ability to conquer the Lie—without actually doubting the Truth itself?

6. How will he overcome this doubt? Will supporting characters encourage him—or will he encourage them?

7. How will you indicate your protagonist's re-dedication of himself to the Truth after his defeat at the Third Plot Point?

8. Can you offer an outright statement of the conflict's foundational "Lie vs. Truth" premise?

9. Why will the Truth be intrinsic to the protagonist's ability to physically defeat the antagonist?

10. How can minor characters' new grip on the Truth support your protagonist's final attack on the Lie without stealing the limelight from him?

11. How will the Resolution prove the changes created by the protagonist and his Truth?

12. Will the world be different from how it was in the beginning—or will the protagonist return to the same world he was originally forced to leave?

13. Which of the supporting characters will manifest the Truth in the Resolution?

14. Will the protagonist demonstrate any exterior or personal differences from who he was at the beginning of the story?

15. How can you reinforce that his core Truth has not changed at all?

The flat "arc" is often misunderstood and sometimes overlooked. Authors often believe something's amiss with their stories because their protagonists aren't changing. But in fact, Flat Character Arcs create some of the most dynamic stories. Strong catalyst characters can be just as flawed and fascinating as can those with the deepest of Change Arcs. But their solid devotion to one foundational Truth gives them the power to create dramatic changes in the world and characters around them. When structured properly, the result can be unforgettable.

PART 3:
THE NEGATIVE
CHANGE ARC

"Lying to ourselves
is more deeply ingrained
than lying to others."
—Fyodor Dostoevsky

18

The First Act

WHO WOULD WANT to write a Negative Arc? Well, how about Shakespeare, Dostoevsky, Faulkner, and Flaubert?

Just to name a few small-time wordsmiths you may have heard tell of.

Everybody likes a happy ending, but, let's face it, not all stories *have* happy endings. Negative Change Arcs won't give readers the warm fuzzies and spawn date-night movie adaptations. But they do have the ability to create stories of unparalleled power and resonance—*if they're true.*

Truth resonates whether it's happy or hard, and some of the hardest truths to swallow are the most important for any of us to understand. That's where your ability to wield the Negative Change Arc will come in handy. The Negative Change Arc tells the story of a character who ends in a worse place than that in which he started—and probably drags others down with him. In *The Moral Premise*, Stanley D. Williams provides this formula for Negative Change Arcs:

> Virtue leads to success, and Vice leads to defeat, but Unrelenting vice leads to destruction.

3 Manifestations of a Negative Arc

There are far more ways to do things wrong than there are ways to do things right (hence my ongoing blog series "Most

Common Writing Mistakes"—which will probably never run out of fodder). So it goes with character arcs. The Positive Change Arc has one basic manifestation. Same for the Flat Arc. But the Negative Change Arc can follow several variations.

Before we dig into the key structural points of the Negative Change Arc's First Act, let's examine three of the possible routes your story's Negative Change Arc may take.

1. The Disillusionment Arc

CHARACTER BELIEVES LIE > OVERCOMES LIE > NEW TRUTH IS TRAGIC

(**Examples:** *The Great Gatsby* by F. Scott Fitzgerald, *Training Day* directed by Antoine Fuqua)

In many ways, the Disillusionment Arc isn't negative at all. Just as in a Positive Change Arc, the protagonist is growing into a better understanding of the Truth. Possibly the character's life will even be changed for the better. And yet the story is still a downer. The character is moving from a positive outlook to a negative one. His new Truth isn't sunshine and roses; it's cold hard facts.

2. The Fall Arc

CHARACTER BELIEVES LIE > CLINGS TO LIE > REJECTS NEW TRUTH > BELIEVES STRONGER/WORSE LIE

(**Examples:** *Wuthering Heights* by Emily Brontë, *Doubt* directed by John Patrick Shanley)

The Fall Arc is the one we most commonly associate with tragedies. In this type of story, the character starts out just as he would in a Positive Change Arc: already entrenched in the Lie. But unlike a Positive Change Arc, in which he will eventually overcome the Lie and embrace the Truth, the protagonist in a Fall Arc will reject every chance for embracing the Truth and will fall more and more deeply into the morass of his own sins—usually dragging others right along with him. His story will end in insanity, oppressive immorality, or death.

3. The Corruption Arc

CHARACTER SEES TRUTH > REJECTS TRUTH > EMBRACES LIE

(**Examples:** *The Godfather* by Mario Puzo, *Star Wars*, Episodes I-III directed by George Lucas)

In a Corruption Arc, the character starts out in a world that already knows and embraces the Truth. He has every opportunity to do the same, but is lured away by the Lie. Just as the seed of the Truth is already latent in the life of a Positive Change Arc character, the seed of the Lie is latent in the Corruption Arc character—even though the Truth is already right in front of him. This is perhaps the most moving of all the arcs, since it features a character who is good—or at least has a great potential for goodness—but who throws away that chance and consciously chooses darkness. In many ways, the Corruption Arc is similar to the Disillusionment Arc, but as William Bernhardt points out in *Perfecting Plot*:

> It's possible to be disillusioned without being corrupted, and it's possible to be corrupted without being disillusioned.

THE LIE THE CHARACTER BELIEVES

Just as in a Positive Change Arc, the Negative Change Arc hinges on the Lie the Character Believes. In a Positive Change Arc, the Lie is about something the character is lacking (e.g., he believes he needs money in order to be happy). In a Negative Change Arc, the Lie is about something the character *already* possesses but devalues (e.g., he's already filthy rich, but he fails to value or be responsible with his blessings). There will be one specific, objectively good thing in his life that he will take for granted. Worse, he will be willing to sacrifice this good thing (and its inherent Truth) in order to pursue the false promise of the Lie. The Thing the Character Wants, the Thing He Needs, and the Ghost will be basically the same in both a Negative Change Arc and a Positive Change Arc. It's only how the character deals with his Ghost over the course of the story that significantly differs—as he falls prey to its power over him, rather than overcoming it.

The Disillusionment Arc Example

The Great Gatsby: Nick Carraway, although only an observer to the larger-than-life antics and pursuits of his eccentrically rich friend Jay Gatsby, is still the main character in this classic novel. He starts out the story as a naïve and optimistic young man from the Midwest. His Lie is a cheerful one: *people—especially rich, beautiful, popular ones—are exactly who they seem, and the lives of the East Egg residents must, therefore, be reaching the pinnacle of happiness.* The Thing He Wants is to be one of them, while the Thing He Needs is to learn the Truth about *the shallowness behind their glittering façades.* His Ghost is essentially his own naïvety, as the result of his unsophisticated upbringing.

The Fall Arc Example

Wuthering Heights: Heathcliff starts out believing the Lie that *in order to ever find personal wholeness or happiness, he must entirely possess his adopted sister, childhood sweetheart, and only friend Cathy Earnshaw.* The Thing He Wants is, of course, Cathy herself. But the Thing He Needs is to let her go and move away from their dangerously obsessive and destructive relationship. His Ghost is his own orphaned (and presumably illegitimate) childhood, in which he is endlessly spurned by everyone except Cathy and her father.

The Corruption Arc Example

Star Wars, Episodes I-III: I'll start off this example by saying what everyone already knows: these movies are, almost entirely, examples of how *not* to do things. However, the one thing they do get right is the basic structure of the fall of Anakin Skywalker in what (in my admittedly biased fangirl opinion) could have been one of the best Corruption Arcs in cinema had it been told within less dismally awful movies. Anakin starts out as an optimistic, hopeful child who brings light and kindness into the lives of all those around him. The Truth he already knows is that *love is stronger than physical power.* But the seed of the Lie is also already within him, fertilized by his Ghost as a repressed and powerless slave. The Thing He Wants Most is to protect and save those he cares about (his mother and, later, his wife), but, as Yoda tells him, the Thing He Needs is to "train yourself to let go of everything you fear to lose."

THE NORMAL WORLD

The manifestation of the Normal World in a Negative Change Arc will depend on which of the variations your story is following. In a **Disillusionment Arc**, the character will start out seeing only the glitter and glamour of the Lie: its false promise of hope and success. As a result, the Normal World of the Lie will seem wonderful and beautiful. At this point, he has no reason *not* to believe in it or want it.

In a **Fall Arc**, the character will already be entrenched in the Lie, comfortably and perhaps apathetically. His Normal World may seem ordinary and even good on the surface, but its cracks show through. The character isn't uncomfortable enough in his Lie to rock the boat, but neither is he completely happy or content. The Normal World is a symbol of the Lie he can't (and won't) escape.

In a **Corruption Arc**, the character will start out in a comparatively wonderful Normal World. His Normal World is already blessed by the Truth. Despite its drawbacks, it offers the character a safe place of happiness and growth.

The Disillusionment Arc Example

The Great Gatsby: Nick's personal Normal World, glimpsed only briefly in backstory, is his calm and boring Midwestern life. That setting quickly shifts to the Normal World of the Lie, in which he is transfixed by the shining whirl of wealth and pleasure found in his cousin Daisy's upscale life in East Egg, New York.

The Fall Arc Example

Wuthering Heights: The very name of Heathcliff's home—Wuthering Heights—underlines the turbulent themes of the story. Brontë writes that "wuthering" describes, "the atmospheric tumult to which its station is exposed in the stormy weather." When Heathcliff is adopted as a boy, he is brought to this severe and barren place, where everyone from the master's son to the staff despises him and treats him with cruelty. Only his doomed adopted father and the unruly Cathy accept him. Heathcliff despises everyone else right back, but his almost supernatural bond with Cathy holds him in this hellish existence.

The Corruption Arc Example

Star Wars: On its exterior, Anakin's Normal World as greedy Watto's slave on Tatooine is less than great. But his skills as a mechanic and pilot mean he and his mother are treated well. They live happily together, content in each other's love.

THE CHARACTERISTIC MOMENT

As in the Positive and Flat Arcs, the primary function of a Negative Change Arc's Characteristic Moment is to introduce the character's true self. This encompasses more than just the character's personality and focus (both of which are important). It also needs to hint at the character's *potential*, specifically as it pertains to his relationship with the Lie. Even if the character starts out as a perfectly likable chap who helps little old ladies across the street, readers still need to gain an almost immediate sense of the dark nature that will lead to his doomed future.

The Disillusionment Arc Example

The Great Gatsby: An older, wiser Nick looks back on his adventures with Gatsby by sharing some advice his father used to give him, "Whenever you feel like criticizing any one [*sic*], just remember that all the people in this world haven't had the advantages you've had." The sublime irony here, as readers will discover, is that Nick and his somewhat weary contempt are the products of a "Midwestern" town, which at first glance has none of the benefits of Gatsby's wicked and glamorous city. We are immediately given a sense of the naïvety with which Nick starts out the story, as well as the poignant cynicism with which he will end it.

The Fall Arc Example

Wuthering Heights: Just as in *The Great Gatsby*, readers' first glimpse of Heathcliff comes late in the chronological narrative, almost at the very end. He is already a grown man, misanthropic, cruel, and long scarred by his devotion to his Lie. A few chapters later, we see him at the beginning of his own story, when Mr. Earnshaw first brings him, as a boy, to Wuthering Heights. He is introduced as a silent, long-suffering child, who craves love (the maid finds him huddled on the cold floor in front of Mr. Earnshaw's bedroom door the next morning), but who also seems to have the capability for great violence and passionate cruelty.

The Corruption Arc Example

Star Wars: Anakin is introduced in his role as a slave. He immediately imparts the sense that he is someone who understands Truths about life. He is centered, happy, generous, and kind. But the Lie pokes out around the corners, in his occasional angry retorts to those who hold power over him (Watto and Sebulba). He voices his discontentment with his lot and his determination to protect his mother when he tells Qui-Gon he dreams of becoming a Jedi and returning to free all the slaves by force.

THE FIRST ACT

As in any type of character arc, the Negative Change Arc's First Act must be spent developing both the Truth and the Lie. Whenever either the Truth or the Lie is on stage, the other is there as well, if only by reflection. In all of the Negative Change Arc's variations, the Lie gets precedence over the Truth. Readers need to understand how the Lie has shaped the protagonist's world and how he relates to it personally.

Just as importantly, you must establish the stakes. What is at stake for everyone in the story if the protagonist pursues the Lie? What must he sacrifice if he chooses the Truth over the Lie? Don't make the choices too black and white. Whenever a character makes an important decision, it should be a difficult one. Whatever he chooses, he will have to sacrifice something of great value. Likewise, whatever he chooses, he will also gain something of great value.

The character won't yet have the insight necessary to name either the Truth or the Lie. He has no idea he's dealing with anything so grand. All he knows is that he's being presented with choices. Something in his life isn't quite right, and he wants to make it better, one way or the other. His first major decision and action—which will force him out of his Normal World—won't happen until the end of the First Act. Up until that point, spend your time upping the ante on his personal discomfort and leading him to the opportunities that will set his feet on the path away from the Truth.

The Disillusionment Arc Example

> **The Great Gatsby:** Nick spends the First Act being introduced to high society, with varying levels of success. He

hangs out with his cousin Daisy and her brutish husband Tom, is introduced to Tom's ill-fated relationship with the mechanic George Wilson and his bombshell wife Myrtle, and meets his own fling Jordan Baker. Gatsby doesn't show up in the First Act, but his presence looms large as the light among lights in this glittering landscape. We particularly get the sense of a history between Gatsby and Daisy.

The Fall Arc Example

Wuthering Heights: Throughout the First Act, we are shown Heathcliff's devotion to his Lie (*that he needs Cathy*), as they grow up together, sheltering each other from the cruel world around them. As far as it goes, it would seem that Heathcliff *does* need Cathy and that there's nothing wrong with that. But we also get a front-row seat to Cathy's violently selfish and unpredictable behavior. Even Cathy herself begins to disdain Heathcliff's devotion after she gets a taste of a more refined world while convalescing with their neighbors the Lintons. She begins to accept Edgar Linton's romantic advances, not because she loves him, but because she wants to be rich and refined. Even though she adores Heathcliff and defends him against her brother and others, she treats him abominably. Readers come to understand that Heathcliff would be much better off if only he could break his eerie bond with her.

The Corruption Arc Example

Star Wars: The entirety of Episode I is essentially the First Act in this arc. As such, it shows both Anakin's potential for goodness, but also his potential for great power. As long as he is in the Normal World with his mother, he clings to the Truth. But he is tempted away from that Truth by Qui-Gon's promises that he could learn to wield great power as a Jedi. He craves the power both as a solution toward freeing his mother, but also as an antidote to the powerlessness he has lived with all his life. When the Jedi Council briefly threatens his dream, we see the hold the Lie is already coming to have over him.

QUESTIONS TO ASK ABOUT THE FIRST ACT IN A NEGATIVE CHANGE ARC

1. Will your protagonist fulfill a Disillusionment Arc, a Fall Arc, or a Corruption Arc?

2. What Lie will your character fall prey to?

3. How does this Lie manifest in the beginning of your story?

4. How does the Truth manifest in the character (in a **Disillusionment Arc**) or in the world around him in?

5. How is the character devaluing the Truth in the beginning of the story?

6. What Ghost is influencing the character's belief in or proclivity toward the Lie?

7. What is the Thing the Character Needs?

8. What is the Thing the Character Wants?

9. If you're using a **Disillusionment Arc**, why does the Lie's Normal World appeal to the character?

10. If you're using a **Fall Arc**, how is the character already entrenched in the Lie's Normal World? Why has he not yet made a move to escape this Normal World?

11. If you're using a **Corruption Arc**, how is the character's Normal World nourished by the Truth? Why is the character still less than comfortable in this world?

12. How can you use the Characteristic Moment to introduce your character's proclivity toward the Lie?

13. What is at stake for the character if he chooses to follow the Lie?

14. What is at stake for the character if he chooses to follow the Truth?

A well-crafted Negative Change Arc provides readers with a protagonist who reveals interesting truths both about the world and about readers *themselves*. Negative Change Arcs are rarely comfortable, but they are important. It's no mistake that so many of the greatest and most memorable stories in literature are tragedies. As readers, we resonate with characters who follow the Lie—and pay for it—because it is a cycle we repeat so often in our own lives. When structured properly to gain maximum resonance, a Negative Change Arc can present sober realities that inspire great change in the world around us.

"People say they love truth,
but in reality they want to believe
that which they love is true."
—Robert J. Ringer

19

THE SECOND ACT

THE SECOND ACT in a Negative Change Arc bears a lot of similarity to that in a Positive Change Arc. In both types of arc, the character will be thrust out of his Normal World into a new and strange dilemma, where he will be forced to confront his Lie. He'll be learning more about that Lie and be given opportunities to recognize its power over him.

So what's the major difference between the Second Act in a Negative Change Arc and the Second Act in a Positive Change Arc?

You guessed it: the character becomes increasingly enthralled by the darkness, rather than overcoming it. In the Negative Change Arc's Second Act, the character will make a series of decisions—the most notable of which will be those at the First Plot Point and the Midpoint—which will cement his enslavement to the Lie.

THE FIRST PLOT POINT

Because Negative Change Arcs are about a descent into darkness, they have to begin in a place high enough for the story to descend *from*. As a result, the First Plot Point will frequently be a positive one. Something seemingly good or interesting happens to the character. He meets the girl of his dreams; he gets a new job; he escapes from a bad situation. He may even make a good decision, one with the potential to lead him *away* from his Lie.

But no matter how comparatively positive the First Plot Point may seem, it must always be dogged by the portent of bad things to come. Foreshadowing must be wielded deftly in a Negative Change Arc more than in any other. If an unhappy ending is going to resonate with readers, they must be prepared for it. They must feel it was the only logical outcome.

The Disillusionment Arc Example

The Great Gatsby: Gatsby's infamous party is a suitably glorious First Plot Point. On a thematic level, it aces the symbolism of the glittering corruption of the wealthy East Egg world into which country boy Nick Carraway is being lured. But even more importantly, its introduction of the strange and marvelous Jay Gatsby himself throws open the door that will usher Nick out of the Normal World. At the moment, all looks well. Gatsby and his world seem wonderful, and Nick is delighted to strike up a friendship with him. He makes the *decision* to attend the party—the decision that will change his life.

The Fall Arc Example

Wuthering Heights: After Cathy accepts her neighbor Edgar Linton's marriage proposal, Heathcliff overhears her telling the news to the maid. Cathy admits she doesn't love Edgar—that, indeed, she would be miserable even in heaven if Heathcliff were not there—but that she can't degrade herself to marry Heathcliff because he is so "low." Heathcliff silently leaves, determined to make something of himself so he can return to marry Cathy. His decision is an entirely positive one. He wants to rise above his circumstances, leave behind the tyranny of Cathy's brother Hindley, and claim Cathy's hand as an equal. But readers also sense the darkness that threatens in his actions—especially since Cathy shows no sign of changing her mind about marrying Edgar.

The Corruption Arc Example

Star Wars: If we look at the overall arc of Anakin Sky-walker, apart from the divisions of the movies themselves, we can see that the First Plot Point comes at the end of Episode I when Obi-Wan reluctantly agrees to take Anakin as his apprentice. As a result of this decision, Anakin officially leaves behind the last vestiges of his Normal World as a slave on Tatooine and enters his new world as a Jedi Padawan on Coruscant. This is, on its surface, a very positive move for young Anakin. He's getting the opportunity to learn more about himself and his abilities, as well as the galaxy around him. Lucas's foreshadowing could have been stronger here, but we did get the sense (earlier in Episode I when Anakin gives Mace Windu the evil eye after he's initially rejected by the Jedi Council) that this decision could end up going very wrong.

THE FIRST HALF OF THE SECOND ACT

As always, the First Half of the Second Act is all about the character's reaction to the First Plot Point. He's deliberately moving forward toward the Thing He Wants Most, but he's at a disadvantage in some way. Usually, this is because he lacks complete information about his antagonist or the goal itself. But sometimes the disadvantage can also be the result of the character's own unwillingness to fight out the battle to the last full measure. He may not yet be ready to do *whatever it takes* to win.

He's also learning more about the Lie and the Truth. In a **Disillusionment Arc**, he's encountering difficulties in pursuing the Lie, even as he's getting closer to the Thing He Wants while simultaneously getting farther away from the Thing He Needs.

In a **Fall Arc**, he will be getting a full-on lesson in the Truth. He's going to be suffering as a result of the Lie. He's not getting the Thing He Wants, and, what's more, he's getting slapped for even trying. He's going to have moments when he rethinks his devotion to the Lie, but he wants his story goal too badly to let it go.

In a **Corruption Arc**, the character is going to be learning more and more about the power of the Lie. He recognizes it, if only subconsciously, as a path toward the Thing He Wants. As his obsession with the Thing He Wants increases, he begins more and more to embrace the Lie and reject the Truth.

The Disillusionment Arc Example

The Great Gatsby: Nick spends the First Half of the Second Act getting to know Gatsby and falling under his spell. Gatsby has certainly been corrupted by his lifestyle just as Daisy and the others have been. But he's also different from the others. There's a core of purity amidst his almost childlike hope, and in recognizing the differences between Gatsby and those around him, Nick begins to see the prevalent falsity in the East Egg world. Even still, Nick is being pulled into that corruption by Gatsby himself, as Gatsby introduces Nick to his underworld associates such as Meyer Wolfsheim and convinces Nick to help him arrange a meeting with his lost love Daisy Buchanan.

The Fall Arc Example

Wuthering Heights: Years later, Heathcliff returns as a gentleman, only to discover Cathy has already married Edgar Linton. Feeling betrayed, he fights to overcome his love for her and embrace the Truth that he's better off without her. Still, he clings to her, even though part of him hates her for being untrue to both him and herself. His dark nature comes swarming out as he begins enacting his vengeance against Hindley (by encouraging his gambling and drinking) and against Edgar (by marrying his sister Isabella).

The Corruption Arc Example

Star Wars: Now an adult, Anakin falls in love with Senator Padmé Amidala, even though it violates his oaths as a Jedi apprentice. He is passionate about being a Jedi and the power it allows him to wield, but he also resents the rules the Jedi Order enforce in his life. He rebels against them and allows his romance with Padmé to flourish, hoping he can hold onto both the Thing He Wants and the Thing He Needs.

THE MIDPOINT

The Midpoint is where it all changes. Up to this point, the character has been advancing toward his Lie, but the advance has been slow—and certainly not irreversible. He's had *at least* a few moments where he's been torn about the course he's following. But at the Midpoint, he takes an irremediable action or experiences a blindingly clear revelation that will see him launching himself into the second half with a series of strong Lie-based actions.

The Midpoint needs to feature a moment in which the character is clearly presented with the Truth and the opportunity to follow it.

The Disillusionment Arc Example

The Great Gatsby: After helping Gatsby arrange a strangely manic reunion with Daisy, Nick begins to learn the truth about Gatsby's past. This glorious man, adored by all, is a phony. Nick grows impatient with Gatsby's shenanigans, especially his insistence that he can repeat his romantic past with the fickle Daisy. In seeing through the cracks of even Gatsby—easily the best of the East Egg lot—Nick's illusions about the beauty of this upper-class world begin to crumble.

The Fall Arc Example

Wuthering Heights: When Cathy dies in childbirth after a long illness, Heathcliff is offered a Moment of Truth; with Cathy now forcibly removed from his life, he is given the opportunity to accept the Truth that *he's better off without her.* But he not only throws aside the Truth, he embraces a new and more horrible Lie: *he would rather have Cathy's ghost haunt him and drive him insane than give her up.*

The Corruption Arc Example

Star Wars: Anakin argues for a secret relationship with Padmé in defiance of his vows to the Jedi, but Padmé resists, insisting she couldn't live a lie. In that instance, Anakin experiences a Moment of Truth, in which he recognizes the correctness of her words ("You're right. It would destroy us") and struggles to acquiesce to them. But after yet another nightmare about his captured mother, he takes a huge step away from controlled acceptance into the chaos of his own power when he decides to disobey his orders and return to Tatooine to rescue her.

THE SECOND HALF OF THE SECOND ACT

After his revelation and his rejection of the Truth at the Midpoint, the character will now begin actively and aggressively pursuing the Thing He Wants in the Second Half of the Second Act. Although he will still experience glimmers of the Truth (particularly in the form of resistance and reprimands from supporting characters), he has already cast off its fetters. The Truth is no longer a personal obstacle between him and his Lie-driven goal.

The exception to this is, of course, the **Disillusionment Arc**, which sees the character growing *into* the Truth, just as he would in a Positive Change Arc—the difference between the two being the destructive negativity of the Disillusionment Arc's Truth.

The tragic premise indicates a progression from bad to worse. Whatever the character's Lie in the beginning, he will now begin growing into its worst manifestation. If he fought lust in the story's beginning, he will now descend into adultery or even rape. If he struggled with hatred, he may end up plotting a murder.

The Disillusionment Arc Example

The Great Gatsby: Nick becomes more and more (you guessed it!) disillusioned and disgusted with the lives of his rich friends. He watches Daisy engage in an affair with the obsessively and almost innocently hopeful Gatsby, while her hypocritical husband stews behind the scenes. Nick closes out the Second Act with an observation on his thirtieth birthday: "Before me stretched the portentous menacing road of a new decade." Quite a change of mindset for the optimistic boy from the country.

The Fall Arc Example

Wuthering Heights: After Cathy's death, Heathcliff lashes out in anger, punishing everyone who had anything to do with keeping him away from her. He coerces his adopted brother Hindley into drunken gambling that allows Heathcliff to gain the deed to Wuthering Heights—and then he allows Hindley to drink himself to death. He shows no care for his own pregnant wife—Isabella Linton—and lets her flee to another town. He raises Hindley's son Hareton in as abject degradation as he himself was raised. And, as the years go by, he plots to marry his sickly son Linton to Edgar and Cathy's daughter Catherine, so that he can gain control of a dying Edgar's property as well.

The Corruption Arc Example

Star Wars: After his mother dies in his arms, Anakin takes a huge step toward the Dark Side when he murders every person—man, woman, and child—in the Sand People's village. He then consistently and obsessively chooses to protect Padmé over any and all practical or moral restraints—losing an arm and nearly sacrificing his master in the process. He secretly marries her in defiance of his vows and, as time goes by, proves himself willing to seek answers even from the Dark Side in order to save her from dying in childbirth.

QUESTIONS TO ASK ABOUT THE NEGATIVE CHANGE ARC IN THE SECOND ACT

1. What is your character's great fault in the beginning of your story (e.g., lust, hatred, etc.)?

2. How does the First Plot Point initially seem to be a good thing?

3. How is the character's eventual descent foreshadowed even amid the positive aspects of the First Plot Point?

4. In the First Half of the Second Act, what is hampering the character from gaining the Thing He Wants Most?

5. If you're writing a **Disillusionment Arc**, what is your character learning about the Lie in the First Half of the Second Act?

6. If you're writing a **Fall Arc**, how is your character suffering for his devotion to the Lie?

7. If you're writing a **Corruption Arc**, why is your character growing more and more enamored with the Lie?

8. At the Midpoint, what Moment of Truth gives your character an opportunity to embrace the Truth? Why and how does he reject it?

9. How is your character actively and aggressively using the Lie to pursue the Thing He Wants in the Second Half of the Second Act?

10. In the Second Half of the Second Act, how is the character evolving into the worst possible manifestation of his initial great fault?

The Second Act is the heart of the Negative Change Arc. The First Act is all about setting up the place from which he falls, and the Third Act is all about showing the place *to* which he falls. But the Second Act is where the falling happens. This is the meaty, chewy stuff that proves your story's Lie and Truth and convinces readers of the realism of your character's devolvement. Write a killer Second Act, and your Negative Change Arc will rock readers' worlds.

"Woe, destruction, ruin, and decay;
the worst is death and death will have his day."
—William Shakespeare

20

THE THIRD ACT

I N ONE WORD, the Negative Change Arc is about *failure*. This becomes nowhere more clear than in the Third Act. If the Positive Change Arc is about *redeeming self* and the Flat Arc is about *saving others*, then the Negative Change Arc is about *destroying self and probably others as well*.

The previous two acts have been all about the setup for that inevitable destruction. The character has been making active choices, but since they've all been based on the false foundation of the Lie, they've turned out to be horribly wrong choices. Unlike Positive Change Arc characters, who will make mistakes but will then recognize and learn from those mistakes, the Negative Change Arc character will refuse to even recognize his mistakes, much less embrace opportunities to grow past them and rectify them.

The result is a story that's horrifyingly resonant in its recognizableness. Negative Change Arcs act as cautionary tales for readers, since none of us want to end up as tragic heroes. But these stories' great power is not in their "moral," but rather in their sheer familiarity. We all play out Negative Change Arcs over and over in our own lives (although hopefully on smaller stages than Gatsby, Heathcliff, and Anakin). We know how thin the wire we're all balancing on and how easy it is to fall off and end up dogmatically determined to believe that the Lies we've lived haven't been mistakes.

THE THIRD PLOT POINT

No matter what type of arc you're writing, the Third Plot Point is always a place that reeks of death. The character is brought face to face with his mortality—either because his own life is threatened (literally or by extension, as when, for example, his livelihood or good name is under siege) or because the lives of those he cares about are put under the axe. In Positive and Flat Arcs, the character will face down death, come to terms with its power, re-embrace life, and rise ready to once again do battle.

But in a Negative Change Arc, the protagonist will find himself impotent in the face of this horror. The Lie he has stubbornly embraced throughout the story now renders him powerless. In essence, he's lacking the one weapon—the Truth—necessary to fight and defeat the Lie. His only option is to surrender himself still deeper into the grip of the Lie in an effort to convince himself he has chosen the right path.

As always, the exception to the rule is the Disillusionment Arc, in which the character *will* face and accept the Truth. But it is a dark and horrifying Truth.

The Disillusionment Arc Example

> *The Great Gatsby*: The Third Plot Point begins with a showdown between Gatsby and Daisy's husband Tom, in which Tom reveals to Daisy that Gatsby has earned his money through criminal activities such as bootlegging. Daisy wavers from her decision to run away with Gatsby, and Tom orders Gatsby to drive her home. As Tom, Nick, and Jordan follow in a second car, they encounter a tremendous accident. They learn Gatsby's yellow roadster hit and killed Tom's mistress Myrtle. Nick is mostly an observer to these dramatic happenings, but they have brought him to a growing disgust for the entire East Egg set and their underhanded dealings with one another.

The Fall Arc Example

Wuthering Heights: Heathcliff kidnaps Edgar and Cathy's teenage daughter Catherine and refuses to let her return to her dying father unless she marries Heathcliff's son Linton. She finally complies and rushes home to her father just in time to watch him die. Heathcliff has achieved his great end—as many tragic protagonists do—by completing his vengeance. He has destroyed Edgar: his enemy is dead, and Heathcliff now holds title to all his property. But his victory has brought him no closer to peace—or to his true goal of being with Cathy.

The Corruption Arc Example

Star Wars: The Third Plot Point in Anakin's arc is the moment when he realizes he cannot allow Mace Windu and the other Jedi Masters to kill the Sith Lord Darth Sidious. His desperate need to protect his wife, no matter the cost, prompts him to save the life of the man who has already killed millions and will kill millions more. More than that, he surrenders himself as an apprentice to the Dark Side, in order to learn Sidious's secrets of life and death.

THE THIRD ACT

After the breaking point at the Third Plot Point, the tragic hero will rage futilely against death and its power, rather than rising into a personal resurrection. In *45 Master Characters*, Victoria Lynn Schmidt writes:

He isn't at all humbled by his experience: In fact, he builds up his own ego trying to prove he's more than a mere human being. He may take risks without thinking and will demand to fight the villain alone. He's like a one-man show ... who doesn't need anyone or anything. He won't face what the [antagonist] is showing him [about the Truth]. He won't look inside himself to find out what he really wants out of life.

Without the Truth, he has no tools with which to cope with this new tragedy. As a result, he spends the first half of the Third Act (prior to the Climax) determined to strike out at the antagonistic force and reach for the Thing He Wants *any way he can.* He will commit any number of crimes and sins. He has nothing left to lose and no moral compass to guide him.

Supporting characters may try to reason with him, but he will now be even less open to their suggestions. He may even turn on people whom he was previously willing to accept despite their differing opinions. He simply has too much invested in his present course; he can't afford to be talked out of it, even at the cost of alienating those he would previously have fought and died for. The end is entirely outweighing the means it costs to achieve it.

The Disillusionment Arc Example

> *The Great Gatsby***:** After refusing to go with Jordan into the Buchanans' house (in essence, refusing to join their corrupt lifestyle), Nick encounters Gatsby and learns the truth of the drive-by accident: Gatsby wasn't driving at all; Daisy was. Fearing Tom may harm Daisy, Gatsby insists on taking the blame for the accident and remains outside the Buchanans' house all night. By now, the dark Truth has dawned for Nick. He knows too well that Tom and Daisy are one of a kind. Daisy will let Gatsby take the blame, even as she distances herself from him without a second thought—not because remaining with her husband is the right thing to do but because she selfishly knows it's in her best interest. Nick finally and conclusively realizes the East Egg crowd is a "rotten bunch." He sticks around to try to help Gatsby, but from that point on, he's no longer bewitched by the spectacles of wealth and beauty.

The Fall Arc Example

> *Wuthering Heights***:** After the completion of his vengeance against Edgar, Heathcliff sinks deeper and deeper

into despair. He is broken, and he can't find the strength to rise above his continuing obsessive need to be with Cathy. He even goes so far as to dig up her long-rotted corpse, and he does find momentary peace in the belief that it will be his soul—and not Edgar's—that will be reunited with her in death. After his own son dies, he drifts through life, torturing Catherine and Hindley's son Hareton and contemplating Cathy's ghost, who he believes has finally returned to haunt him. The only possible remaining route to his goal is death itself.

The Corruption Arc Example

Star Wars: Believing the Dark Side is the only possible solution to saving his wife, Anakin throws himself into the darkness completely. Even as he mourns the atrocities his new master orders him to commit, he doesn't flinch from them. He can't afford to. He's come too far. The hole is too deep, and there's no way back up. His only chance for himself and his wife is to dig deeper still. After Mace Windu's death, Anakin slaughters the Jedi, young and old alike, as well as the Separatist Coalition—and anyone else who gets in his and his new master's way.

THE CLIMAX

The Climax is where everything finally and fully falls apart. The character's last desperate push to use the Lie to gain the Thing He Wants will achieve one of two possible outcomes:

1. He gains an apparent outer victory, in which he is able to claim the Thing He Wants, but in which his success is a hollow one. Without the Truth he can never find inner wholeness by gaining the Thing He Needs. In this type of ending, the Climactic Moment will likely include a glimpse of the Truth, in which the character comes to the crushing realization that his battle was a wasteful one and, worse, that the outrages he's committed along the way have destroyed both himself and everything he once loved.

2. He loses both the inner and the outer battle. His inability to equip himself with the Truth dooms him to failure in his final conflict.

In planning the Climax in a Negative Change Arc, look back at the person your character was in the beginning of the book. The Lie he struggled with in the beginning—and the way in which he struggled with it—should point you to an obvious culmination in the Climax.

The Disillusionment Arc Example

The Great Gatsby: Nick's disillusionment is complete when Gatsby is murdered by Myrtle's husband—who believed Gatsby was responsible for her death and who then kills himself. All the people who flocked to Gatsby and his parties during his life disappear upon word of his death. Only a handful of mourners, Nick among them, attend his funeral.

The Fall Arc Example

Wuthering Heights: As Catherine and Hareton begin to fall in love, Heathcliff is troubled by how closely their relationship mirrors his own youthful past with Cathy. His belief that Cathy is haunting him grows stronger and stronger, and he finds a measure of manic happiness in her supposed presence. His health declines rapidly as the result of his nightly walks on the moors, until one morning Hareton finds him dead. He has gone at last to be with Cathy, in the only possible way they could ever be together—by embracing the Lie more fully in the end than even at the beginning.

The Corruption Arc Example

Star Wars: Anakin's wife Padmé and former master Obi-Wan rush to stop him. When Padmé rejects Anakin's methods for trying to save her, he lashes out at her.

Even though keeping her alive has been the reason for his horrific choices and actions, he has now come too far down his dark path to brook resistance even from her. He nearly kills her, then turns on Obi-Wan and is eventually brutally wounded as a result of his blind faith in his own power.

THE RESOLUTION

The ending scenes in a tragedy are often comparatively short. Unlike a positive story, Negative Change Arcs leave few loose ends and don't usually inspire in readers a desire to stick around in the story world. The great tragedy in the Climax is underscored with a sense of finality that doesn't require much mopping up.

Still, some small postscript is almost always necessary. In the event of your protagonist's death, you'll need to show the surviving characters' reactions, especially since many of them will probably have undergone Disillusionment Arcs as a result of witnessing his fall. You'll want to show the effect of the protagonist's actions upon the world around him. Presumably, he's left it a worse place than that in which it started, but you may want to hint at the possibility for new hope in the world now that the protagonist's dark influence has been lifted.

Most important, you'll want to create a closing scene that drives home the character's final state. Death, insanity, war, destruction, imprisonment—whatever finds him in the end should be represented in the story's closing motif, as a clear contrast to how the story began.

The Disillusionment Arc Example

The Great Gatsby: After the funeral, Nick distances himself from the East Egg crowd. Blinders now removed, he finds little to appreciate in the city life he once loved. He decides to return home, but not without officially ending his relationship with Jordan and confronting Tom. He revisits Gatsby's house, where the grass is now overgrown, and he once again compares Gatsby, with his sense of wonder and hope, to the cynicism and selfishness of the world that destroyed him.

The Fall Arc Example

Wuthering Heights: Without Heathcliff's dark presence to poison their lives, Catherine and Hareton begin at last to bring love and happiness back into the corrupted atmosphere of Wuthering Heights. The book closes on an entirely hopeful note, promising the end of suffering. There's even a hint of hope for Heathcliff, as the old manservant insists he can see his master's ghost walking the moors with Cathy. The narrator, however, gives his own spin on a hopeful end for Heathcliff, believing that in death, at least, he will find rest.

The Corruption Arc Example

Star Wars: Anakin's efforts are completely ruined in the aftermath of his climactic fall. Just as he feared, his wife dies in childbirth—but, ironically, as the result of his own actions. He is rescued from death by his new master and confined to life as a monstrous cyborg. His story, of course, continues with the promise of "a new hope" in the galaxy.

QUESTIONS TO ASK ABOUT THE NEGATIVE CHANGE ARC IN THE THIRD ACT

1. How will your character fail in the story's end?

2. How will his actions irrevocably damage others?

3. What tragedy will confront your protagonist at the Third Plot Point?

4. How will your character react to the Third Plot Point?

5. Why does your character's refusal to embrace the Truth render him powerless to rise from the Third Plot

Point better equipped to deal with both his inner and outer conflict?

6. What less-than-ideal (and possibly even downright evil) plan will your protagonist come up with for confronting the antagonistic force and gaining the Thing He Wants?

7. Will supporting characters try to reason with your protagonist? How will he respond?

8. In the Climax, will your character gain the Thing He Wants? If so, why will he realize his victory is still a hollow one? How will he react?

9. Alternatively, will your character fail to gain his ultimate goal? How will he react?

10. After his failure in the Climax, will your character at least momentarily realize the Truth and confront the futility of his actions?

11. How are your character's actions in the Climax a magnified reflection of his Lie in the beginning of the story?

12. How does your Resolution show the effect of your protagonist's actions upon supporting characters and the world-at-large?

13. Will you end on a hopeful note or a despairing note? Why?

14. How does your closing scene underline the character's ultimate failure?

We often think of Negative Change Arcs as depressing, and, indeed, sometimes they are. But they're also exceedingly necessary, just as vinegar is necessary to cleanse the palate after too much sugar. Tell your Negative Change Arcs boldly. As long as you remember the unique structural turning points and the proper progression of pacing and foreshadowing, you'll be able to create a Negative Change Arc every bit as compelling and entertaining as one with a happy ending.

PART 4:
FAQs About
Character Arcs

"You need to know the characters as living, breathing people before you start the plot; otherwise, you'll feel panic, anarchy and chaos."
—Deborah Moggach

21

How Can I Figure Out What My Character's Arc Should Be?

YOU NOW KNOW how to structure your character's arc—whether it's Positive, Flat, or Negative. But what you may still be wondering is how to figure out *which* arc you should choose for your character.

Choosing your character's arc is every bit as important a decision as choosing the right plot. Get it wrong in the beginning, and, at best, you'll be facing massive rewrites. Some stories will pop into your brain with an obvious character arc already intact. But other stories will require a little more forethought. Fortunately, picking the perfect character arc for your story requires nothing more than the answers to three questions.

1. What's Your Genre?

Genre won't *always* be the deciding factor in the type of character arc you portray, but it should definitely be a consideration. As Harold Crick learned in *Stranger Than Fiction*, stories follow certain patterns: "Tragedy you die. Comedy you get hitched." Positive Change Arcs get happy endings. Negative Change Arcs get sad endings.

Broader "umbrella" genres such as fantasy, westerns, and historicals can tell just about any kind of story. But most romances, for example, are going to require a Positive Change or Flat Arc.

2. WHERE DOES YOUR CHARACTER'S ARC BEGIN?

Character arc is always *the final sum of your story's ending minus your story's beginning.*

If you can figure out who your character is in the beginning of your story, you're already halfway to writing his arc.

Is he in a comparatively good place in the beginning?

If so, then he's either in a **Flat Arc** (in which he'll have to leave that good place and fight for it when it is threatened) or a **Disillusionment** or **Corruption Arc** (in which he will leave the good place and never return).

Or is he in a less-than-good place? If so, he's either in a **Positive Change Arc** (in which he'll journey toward a better place) or a **Fall Arc** (in which things get even worse).

Even more importantly, what does your character believe in the beginning?

If he starts out believing a Lie about himself or the world around him, then he's either at the beginning of a **Positive Change Arc** (in which he'll overcome the Lie and reach a positive Truth), a **Disillusionment Arc** (in which he'll overcome the Lie and reach a negative Truth), or a **Fall Arc** (in which he'll never grow into the Truth, but instead embrace an even worse Lie).

If he believes the Truth, then he's starting out on either a **Flat Arc** (in which he'll use that Truth to transform the world around him) or a **Corruption Arc** (in which he'll fall away from that Truth).

3. WHERE DOES YOUR CHARACTER'S ARC END?

This brings us right back to the old "happy ending or sad ending?" question. If you know your character starts out believing a Lie, but ends up happy, then you know he's going to be following a **Positive Change Arc**.

In other words, a story with a **Positive Change Arc** will always end with the character in the opposite situation to the one in which he found himself in the beginning. The character will have changed, and the world around him will reflect that.

Same goes for a **Negative Change Arc**, but in reverse. Characters in **Disillusionment** and **Corruption Arcs** will end in a place that's a darker reflection of their beginning, while characters in **Fall Arcs** will end up in a place that's the same as the beginning, only worse.

Flat Arc characters won't change personally, but the world and the characters around them will be drastically different from how they were in the beginning of the story.

DOUBLE CHECK YOUR CHARACTER'S ARC

Based on your answers to these three questions, you should be able to identify which arc you want your character to follow and start plotting accordingly. But before you rev your engines too much, stop a moment to double check yourself with the following questions:

1. Is the arc you've identified your strongest possible option?

2. Do your story's beginning and ending contrast each other strongly enough?

3. If your protagonist had to face the events of the Climax in the beginning of the story, would he react to them in the same way he does at the end?

If he would take pretty much the same action at both the beginning and end of the story, you know his Change Arc isn't strong enough.

This holds true for Flat Arcs as well. Although the character's personal Truth and integrity may hold fast throughout the story, he shouldn't have the motive or understanding to act in the same way at the beginning as he will in the end.

Deciding upon the right character arc is every bit as important as the specific story details of the arc itself once you start plotting. Before you ever put pen to paper, take a moment to figure out your character's arc and make it as strong and memorable as possible.

"Most short stories have but one plot.
The very best, however, have
what I call a plot-and-a-half—
that is, a main plot and a small subplot
that feeds in a twist or
an unexpected piece of business
that adds crunch and flavor
to the story as a whole."
—Elizabeth Sims

22

CAN A CHARACTER'S ARC
BE A SUBPLOT?

YOU'VE WRITTEN AN amazing story. Your prem-
ise is high concept. Your plot structure is brilliant. The
whole thing is killer. But the main character's arc seems
to be, well, lacking. It's there all right. It just doesn't get much
screen time. It's more of a, ahem, subplot.

Is that even possible? Is it *workable*? Or is it a sign that your
story is flabby, shallow, and sure to bore readers?

One of the frequent questions I encounter is: "Can a character's arc be a subplot?"

The short and sweet answer is: Yes. Yes, it can.

Not all stories—especially action-oriented stories—will feature huge character arcs that get all kinds of screen time and
prominently showcase the Lie, the Truth, and the character's
pit stops in between. These stories are no less credible than those
with prominently developed arcs. Indeed, their smaller arcs can
be every bit as powerful as those that get higher billing.

Consider three different instances of character arcs that
might figure better in a subplot than the main plot.

SHALLOW ARCS

Some character arcs are the stuff of legend (harking back
to my earlier examples from *A Christmas Carol*, *True Grit*,

and *Wuthering Heights,* among many others). But some are just background color, there to raise the main character to a higher dimension. They exist in perfect structure, but their major catalyst points are much less defined than they might be. Same goes for the character's arc itself. He may *shift* more than *change.*

This is a frequent option for many action stories. In Marvel's space-opera romp *Guardians of the Galaxy,* protagonist Peter Quill experiences an ever-popular version of the Positive Change Arc, which takes him from immature selfishness to selfless heroism. His Ghost (his mother's death and his abduction), Lie *(the only way to survive is to look out for Number One),* and Truth *(the only way to be a complete and fulfilled person is to care what happens to others)* are all obvious. But they serve more as subtext for the character than as avenues of propulsion for the plot.

This type of subplot usually functions best when it is based on an arc that is already familiar. Quill's journey from loner to savior is arguably the most familiar in modern adventure stories, so most readers can fill in the blanks and feel the arc without needing many blatant examples of the character's evolution.

This is easily the least effective presentation of any character arc, since it offers so little material to play with. But it can still prove useful in adding an extra layer of depth to stories that need to focus primarily on the action.

TANGENTIAL ARCS

The *true* character-arc-as-subplot variation is the tangential arc, in which the character's arc is full and prominent, but is only obliquely related to the main plot. It affects and is affected by the main plot, but only indirectly. For the most part, it can stand on its own, apart from the main adventure, and could conceivably occur as the result of any number of catalysts.

Jurassic Park, which I referenced (and plotted out point by point) in Part 1 about the Positive Change Arc, is a good example. Dr. Grant's Change Arc revolves around his belief in the Lie that *children are annoying.* Over the course of the story, he bonds with Lex and Tim and comes to realize they're worth caring for, even to the point of risking his own life in saving them from the dinosaurs. However, this Change Arc is tangential to the main plot—in which Dr. Grant actually displays a Flat Arc, based on his belief in the Truth that *nature is ungovernable*. If we pulled the subplot from the story, we'd lose a lot of its heart, but the main plot would remain unchanged. The Change Arc itself could have conceivably occurred as the result of any number of non-dinosaur adventures in which Dr. Grant might have found himself having to care for the kids.

Even when writing tangential arcs, strive for a tighter link between the subplot and the plot. The more integral the two, the more prominent your character's arc will be—and the more cohesive your story as a whole. Still, *Jurassic Park* is a good example of how even a dramatically unnecessary Change Arc can be used to improve the overall story.

Extra Arcs

Jurassic Park is also a good example of a story in which the protagonist experiences *two* arcs, one of which is integral to the main plot and the other of which is a subplot. The Flat Arc Dr. Grant shares with Ellie and Dr. Malcolm (centered around the Truth that *nature is ungovernable*) powers the main plot, while his Change Arc is only a prominent subplot.

Extra character arcs will often show up in relationship subplots. They can work extremely well when they play off the Lie/Truth in the main plot by presenting different facets of the same theme. However, this is a technique to be used with caution, since you can easily end up with a sloppy story that's all over the place.

When Can a Character's Arc Be a Subplot?

Stories are usually better off featuring prominent character arcs. Always start off by trying to incorporate your character's arc conspicuously in the main plot. However, length is one factor that may play a role in your decision. The shorter your story, the less room you'll have to play with varied elements—and your character's arc may have to take a backseat. The longer your story, the more depth and dimensions you can explore.

Should you decide to incorporate a character's arc as a subplot, plan it just as thoroughly and specifically as you would if it were in the main plot. Its plot points and revelations may not be as blatant, but they should still be evident subtextually, in order to give your story its greatest possible psychological impact.

Despite their comprehensive requirements, character arcs do offer a lot of flexibility. Consider your story from all angles to figure out how much prominence your character's arc will need to enhance the plot to its full advantage.

"All other characters are in a story
first and foremost because of
the relationship they strike to the protagonist
and the way each helps to
delineate the dimensions
of the protagonist's complex nature."
—Robert McKee

23

WHAT IS AN IMPACT CHARACTER? AND WHY DOES EVERY STORY NEED ONE?

WHEN WE THINK of necessary characters, we tend to come up with obvious choices such as the protagonist, the antagonist, and maybe the mentor, love interest, and sidekick. "Impact character" probably isn't at the top of your list. But it should be. Because you can't create a character arc without one.

"Impact character" is the term coined by *Dramatica* authors Melanie Anne Phillips and Chris Huntley to describe what is just as accurately termed by editor Roz Morris the "*catalyst* character." This is the character who slams into your protagonist, catalyzes him into change, and has a major *impact* on his life.

The impact character is the one who enables, empowers, or sometimes just plain forces another character(s) to change.

Basically, this is a Flat Arc character.

Remember, in a Change Arc, the protagonist himself changes, while, in a Flat Arc, the protagonist changes the world *around* him. In essence, a Flat Arc character *is* the impact character in his story, enabling the Change Arcs of the supporting characters who surround him.

So who is the impact character in Change Arcs? That is, of course, the whole question.

WHAT IS THE IMPACT CHARACTER?

The impact character may be a friend, or he may be a foe. More on that in a minute, but, for now, suffice it that his actual role in the story isn't what qualifies him as the pivotal character in your protagonist's change. So what does?

Think of it this way: If the antagonist represents the story's *outer* conflict, then the impact character represents the *inner* conflict.

Just like the antagonist, the impact character is a conflict-causer. Just like the antagonist, he's at odds with the protagonist. But unlike the antagonist, the conflict isn't necessarily the result of opposing goals. Rather, its core is the opposing *worldviews* of the protagonist and the impact character. The protagonist believes the Lie; the impact character already knows the Truth.

Throughout the story, the protagonist and his blind faith in his Lie are going to keep running smack into the impact character's Truth. The protagonist may want to be left in peace with his Lie, but the impact character's persistent presence keeps churning up the protagonist's awareness of the Truth—and creating internal conflict.

Rochester keeps inspiring Jane Eyre (eventually to his temporary detriment) to view herself as his equal. The Ghosts of Christmas keep prodding Scrooge out of his inveterate miserliness. Mattie Ross keeps dragging compromising lawman Rooster Cogburn onto the road to justice.

The impact character may or may not be actively trying to get the protagonist to see that Truth, but he's going to be there at crucial moments in the story to help the protagonist see the error of his ways. He has the answers the protagonist is looking for (even though the protagonist won't know that at the beginning of the story), and those answers are going to end up being pivotal to the protagonist's ability to conquer the antagonist and the external conflict in his quest for his story goal.

WHO IS THE IMPACT CHARACTER?

As Roz Morris explains in her book *Writing Characters Who'll Keep Readers Captivated*, the impact character can take just about any form within your story:

They might be mentor characters. These are figures who guide the protagonist into a new world, awakening the qualities they need to meet the challenges they must face. Typically they're a coach or a father figure. They sometimes perish when they have fulfilled their role, or in a betraying twist they might turn out to be a formidable antagonist....

Note that just because the impact character understands the specific Truth needed by the protagonist, this does not mean he has all Truths figured out. In some instances, he may be a generally benighted character who actually has way less figured out than the protagonist does—except when it comes to this one Truth.

Consider a few options. Your story's impact character might be:

1. The antagonist. (Long John Silver in *Treasure Island*)

2. The contagonist. (Tom Doniphon in *The Man Who Shot Liberty Valance*)

3. The mentor. (Kel in *Mistborn*)

4. The sidekick. (Nadine Groot in *Red River*)

5. The love interest. (Mr. Knightley in *Emma*)

6. Present for most of the story. (Raymond Babbitt in *Rain Man*)

7. Present only intermittently, but looming large in the protagonist's mind. (Obi-Wan Kenobi in *Star Wars*)

8. A collective of several characters. (The Radiator Springs townsfolk in *Cars*)

The impact character is the pivot around which your changing character's arc turns. A character can't change without *something* that impacts him by consistently and convincingly conflicting with his belief in the Lie. When planning your character's arc, put the impact character at the top of your to-do list—and watch that arc happen practically on its own!

"Only enemies speak the truth.
Friends and lovers lie endlessly,
caught in the web of duty."
—Stephen King

24

SHOULD ALL MY MINOR CHARACTERS HAVE ARCS?

I F YOUR PROTAGONIST'S character arc has the ability to deepen your story, then just think how much more depth you can create if all your minor characters have arcs! Dizzying concept, isn't it? And it raises the (somewhat trepidatious) question: *Should* all your minor characters have arcs?

It's a fair question. After all, we want all of our supporting characters to be just as dimensional and lifelike as our protagonists. We want them to be the "heroes of their own stories." Doesn't that mean they should all have arcs of their own?

Maybe. But then again, maybe not.

CAN TOO MANY CHARACTER ARCS BE TOO MUCH OF A GOOD THING?

Here's the thing about giving full-fledged arcs to all your minor characters:

You'll go bats.

Seriously. Just the thought of charting a full-on arc for every single character in my latest work-in-progress makes my eyes cross. It's arc overload!

But, then again, faint heart never won fair book contract, right?

Also true. But here's the other thing about giving full arcs to all your minor characters: It's overkill.

Unless you're writing a generational epic with dozens of main characters, then you simply don't need to chart arcs for all your characters. Readers aren't going to notice if *every character* has an arc. Even if they do, they may end up overwhelmed and confused.

Full-fledged arcs are there to guide your plot and theme. To create a tight, well-woven story, every single arc must be *more* than just complete and coherent in its own right. It must *tie together* with every other arc. Very few stories can handle the weight of complexity from more than a handful of full arcs. Just as importantly, very few stories *need* more than a handful of full arcs.

Feel free to breathe a sigh of relief.

MINOR ARCS FOR MINOR CHARACTERS

That said, every prominent minor character *should* have an arc. Just not a *full* arc. Major characters—your protagonist for sure and maybe a few others we'll discuss in just a sec—get major arcs. But minor characters get minor arcs (of all things!).

Basically, a minor arc is just a very condensed version of a full arc. In *Writing Screenplays That Sell*, Michael Hauge directs writers to ask themselves:

> Is there an "arc" to each primary character's story? In other words, do your [antagonist, sidekick, and love interest] all possess clear outer motivations [goals], and are those desires built up and resolved by the end…?

In short, minor arcs require nothing more than the basic framework of any good story (or scene, for that matter!). This is not to say all your minor character arcs must be this sparse. But as you're running through your checklist of story must-haves, at least make sure all prominent minor characters have individual goals, which are met with obstacles/conflict, which are eventually resolved one way or the other by the story's end.

Whether or not these characters must change (positively or negatively) in quest of their personal goals is entirely up to you and the needs of your story. But before you start fleshing out any character, remember all minor character goals must be pertinent to the plot. The more in-depth their arcs, the more obviously those goals must contribute to a cohesive thematic whole.

WHICH MINOR CHARACTERS SHOULD HAVE COMPLETE ARCS?

How can you tell *which* minor characters deserve more than just dinky minor arcs?

Theme. It all comes down to theme.

A protagonist out there alone on a desert island will be able to discover a theme just fine all by his lonesome. But if your story allows you to supply him with a couple key minor characters, you can put them to work in helping you build a more coherent and resonant theme.

How? Consider a few tactics.

Emphasize Your Minor Characters' Different Approaches to Theme

Let's say your protagonist's journey is going to teach him that true respect must be earned by what a person does, rather than by how rich he is or how much social standing he has. Basically, you could sum up your theme as "respect."

You could explore any number of aspects of respect and disrespect: respect of self, respect of superiors, respect of inferiors, etc. Your main character will be focused on one specific aspect of respect. But your minor characters could also each be dealing with their own respect issues. One character might be trying to respect a difficult authority figure. Another might be fighting personal demons of guilt in order to hang on to his last shreds of self-respect. And another might believe respect is an illusion and, therefore, might as well be gained by deceiving others.

Allowing each character to approach the subject from a slightly different angle gives you all kinds of material to play with in exploring every aspect of your theme.

Contrast Your Sidekick With Your Protagonist

Sidekicks are characters who are almost wholly supportive of your protagonist. They're along for the ride on the same journey as your protagonist, and they're cheering him along in his pursuit of his goals. Your protagonist and his sidekick character(s) will share many similarities.

But they should also share key differences. It's in these differences that your theme will begin to emerge. These differences can be good or bad. If your protagonist believes only rich people are worthy of respect, your sidekick might believe "it's what you do that defines you." Or if your protagonist believes respect must be earned, his sidekick might be the one who believes it's all right to lie to others in order to trick them into respecting him.

The contrast between the beliefs and actions of these two allies will bring your theme into clearer focus.

Compare Your Antagonist With Your Protagonist

When you think about an antagonist, you're likely to focus on the ways in which he's different from your protagonist. But some of the most important aspects of your story will emerge thanks to the ways in which the antagonist and the protagonist aren't so different at all.

Hauge explains:

> Theme emerges when the hero's similarity to the nemesis [antagonist] and difference from the reflection [sidekick] are revealed.... A nemesis won't necessarily represent some bad quality that the hero also possesses and has to overcome. The similarity between hero and nemesis can involve either a positive or negative characteristic and it can be revealed at the beginning ... at the end, or anywhere in between. The only rule is to find a similarity.

Your protagonist and your antagonist might both have been kids who felt the sting of the societal disrespect that comes from being poor. As a result, they both believe wealth equals respect. That common ground between them creates all kinds of interesting thematic possibilities. Both the temptations your protagonist will be subjected to and the warnings (full of foreshadowing!) about what he could become are rife with thematic subtext.

When you use your characters to illustrate your theme, you not only open up the thematic possibilities, you also allow theme to play out naturally in the story—instead of stating it point-blank and cramming it down readers' throats.

The Antagonist's Arc

Must the antagonist's arc always be a Negative Change Arc? You'd think it would be. After all, he's a negative character. But nope.

Remember, the antagonist's arc will always function as a reflection of the protagonist's arc. It is his similarities, as much as his differences, to the protagonist that define their relationship. But the image is reversed.

The antagonist's arc will *often* be the opposite of the protagonist's. If the protagonist is following a Positive Change Arc, the antagonist can effectively follow a reflective Negative Change Arc, in which he fails to overcome a similar Lie and ends up destroyed instead of saved—as does Inspector Javert, in Victor Hugo's *Les Miserables*, who follows a Disillusionment Arc. He starts out with a *mercy vs. justice* Lie similar to the protagonist Jean Valjean's. But unlike Valjean, when Javert finally faces the Truth, it destroys him.

Your antagonist may also end up following a Flat Arc, in which he clings to his own Truth (very possibly a destructive Truth). This is especially likely if your antagonist is also your impact character.

The Impact Character's Arc

In the last chapter, we talked about how the impact character is the catalyst for all Change Arcs. The impact character can manifest as any one (or more) of your characters—whether mentor, sidekick, or love interest. But, very often, the antagonist himself will function as the impact character.

Whatever character fills the impact role, his arc will be Flat.

He knows a Truth, and he will use that Truth (consciously or subconsciously) to goad the protagonist into overcoming his Lie. If the antagonist is the impact character, then his very opposition to the protagonist's goal will act as a goad. This can be a powerful way to approach the antagonist, since his ability to influence the protagonist so profoundly (even if he may not intend it for the protagonist's good) gives him tremendous weight as a character of complex morality.

Detective Alonzo Harris in Antoine Fuqua's *Training Day* is a great example. He's evil, but he provides so much moral complexity that he ends up jarring the protagonist out of his complacent, idealistic view of the world and into a new, if painful, Truth. In the end, of course, Harris pays for impacting the protagonist's life so profoundly.

CAN MINOR CHARACTERS HAVE MULTIPLE ARCS?

Let's make things even more complicated, shall we? Some of your characters may end up following multiple types of arc. This always comes down to how many Lies and Truths they know in contrast to other characters' Lies and Truths.

For example, because your impact character already understands the Truth your protagonist seeks, he will follow a Flat Arc in this respect. But this doesn't mean he will understand *all* Truths. He may be hanging onto or overcoming Lies of his own. Same goes for your protagonist. He may be a mess when it comes to his central character arc and its Lie. But he may have a different kind of Truth figured out, which he can use to help minor characters in their own Positive Change arcs.

Used with care, multiple arcs can create characters of great depth and complexity. But here's the rule of thumb to always keep in mind: No minor arc can overshadow the protagonist's primary arc.

Your protagonist's arc *is* the story (and if it's not, then he's not the protagonist). All other arcs must be subordinate to that arc. They must *support* that arc and contribute to its specific moral premise.

In other words, all arcs must weave together to create a single tapestry. You can't have one character learning about mercy while another character is figuring out it's important to take care of the planet (unless those subjects end up tying together in some thematic way that is unclear to my brain at this particular moment).

Back to our original question: How many character arcs *should* you plot in your stories?

Give attention to your protagonist, antagonist, sidekick, and love interest. The protagonist could be given a full arc, with the antagonist's arc acting in a subtextually reflective and contrasting role. The impact character(s) will follow smaller, supporting arcs. Every other character will receive, at the least, a thematically pertinent goal, conflict, and resolution.

"Change is hard at first,
messy in the middle,
and gorgeous at the end."
—Robin Sharma

25

How Can I Use Rewards and Punishments to Change My Characters?

HOW DO YOU get your character to change? As simple as this question may seem, it's also a practical and important question that deserves an equally practical answer.

At this point in our journey through character arcs, I hope you're stoked about the potential of well-structured inner journeys for your characters—whether they're Positive Change, Flat, or Negative Change Arcs. Now you can join in the general cheer and roll up your sleeves to implement an awesome Change Arc in your story.

But... how do you get your character to change?

THE *ONLY* WAY TO CREATE ORGANIC CHANGE IN YOUR CHARACTER'S ARC

First step, of course, is to run over your character-arc checklist.

Yep, he's got a Lie making him miserable (or at least less-than-fulfilled in some aspect).

Yep, the ending features a terrific new Truth that's going to make his life or his world so much better.

Yep, all of the plot's structural beats are correctly placed to influence every moment of the arc.

With all that under your belt, how do you now *make* your character change? How do you get him from Point A (the Lie) to Point B (the Truth) in a way that makes sense from the inside out? It's not enough to put a character through all the proper motions of a change. To make it really work, the character must *feel* that change. He must be personally motivated to change.

How do you accomplish that?

Let's just say I hope you've got a nice juicy carrot and a not-so-nice hard stick handy.

USING REWARDS AND PUNISHMENTS TO GET YOUR CHARACTER TO CHANGE

People are motivated by pain and pleasure. We move away from pain and toward pleasure. We move away from what we don't want and toward what we do want. As any parent knows, this means rewards and punishments are highly successful motivational tools. And what are our characters except wayward, recalcitrant children who need to be shown a better way?

In *Character Arcs*, Jordan McCollum explains insightfully:

> When the character's positive choice brings her closer to the post-arc state, the best "reward" in storytelling terms would be to bring her closer to her external goal. When a negative choice backfires, the biggest "punishment" is to take her farther away from her external goal. We slowly force the character to see that her pre-arc beliefs and behaviors will no longer work, and she must try something new.

Every story is defined by what the protagonist wants. This external goal (the Thing He Wants Most) starts out as the story's manifestation of ultimate pleasure (even if the story's *true* source of "pleasure" is really the Thing He Needs Most). Naturally, the character is headed straight toward this font of bliss.

But his Lie keeps getting in his way, especially in the first half of the book, prior to the Moment of Truth at the Midpoint. Every time he makes a Lie-based move, out comes your omnipotent authorial stick to give him a good whack on the backside. Unless the character is a total dope, he's eventually going to get tired of getting spanked and try a new tack—a Truth-based tack.

Only when the character begins to act in harmony with the Truth will he stop being punished and instead begin to be rewarded. This is where you pull out that carrot! The more in sync the character is with the Truth, the greater his reward—the greater his progress toward the Thing He Wants and (more importantly) the Thing He Needs.

How "Yes, But..." Disasters Act as Rewards

Properly structured scenes are split into two segments: action and reaction. The action half will be structured into three parts of its own: goal, conflict, outcome. That outcome is almost always going to be disastrous *or* partially disastrous. We call these partial disasters "yes, but..." disasters. They are disasters in which the character's main scene goal is obstructed, but only partially.

In the first half of your story, your character's Lie-based actions are going to be leading him to a lot of full-on disasters. These disasters are punishments. Every time he aims for his goal in the wrong way, he gets slapped for it. He enters the conflict and comes up wanting every time. But every one of these disasters should be teaching him a single important lesson: his Lie isn't giving him the right tools to get what he wants.

As he begins to search for new ways to avoid disasters and reach his goal, he starts growing into the Truth and gaining more effective tools. As a result, in the second half of the story, he's going to be scoring more and more "yes, but..." disasters. He's still not capable of fully defeating the antagonist and winning the conflict (once he does that, the story is over), but he's getting closer. And the closer he gets, the more he will be rewarded by better results.

Figuring out how to get your character to change is a decision that must be made on the macro level of your entire story—the structure of the plot and how it influences all of the character arc's catalytic moments.

But your ability to get the character to change is also dependent on the micro-level decisions you make in every single scene in your story—punishments for Lie-based actions, rewards for Truth-based actions.

In every scene, take the time to identify your character's guiding principle and make sure he's being appropriately punished and rewarded. The result? You'll end up with a powerful character arc based on realistic motivations and flawless cause and effect.

"Like any core idea, the concept of a character arc was made to be tested. Doing so can often result in fantastic storytelling, so long as the author is deliberately abandoning this facet of storytelling to create a positive result."
—Robert Wood

26

WHAT IF MY STORY HAS NO CHARACTER ARC?

C AN YOU WRITE a story with no character arc? Is that even possible? And, if it is, will the story be doomed to drabness in comparison to those that *do* feature rich character arcs?

These are questions I encounter frequently, and they're absolutely valid. We often think character arc and story are synonymous—but then we go looking for the arcs in favorite stories, by trying to find the character's Lie and Truth, and we sometimes come up short. Are we just blind to the arc the author intended? Or could it be that such a soulless thing (gasp!) as a story with no character arc actually exists?

IS IT POSSIBLE TO WRITE A STORY WITH NO CHARACTER ARC?

In a word: yes. Totally possible. This *is* fiction after all. Anything's possible!

Character arcs are centered on moments in people's lives when they're changing their mindsets, their worldviews, their personal paradigms. But lots of interesting things can happen without radical personal growth having to go along with it.

For example, let me tell you a story about my siblings and me when we were kids.

One of our favorite movies when we were growing up was *The Great Escape*. We'd go out in the backyard and pretend we were POWs, that the picket fence around the yard was the prison walls, and that we had to dig tunnels, evade the guards, and escape—all that fun stuff.

But first we'd have to pick the characters we were going to be. The casting always went down pretty much the same way. I was oldest (and the bossiest) so I got to pick first—which naturally meant that I always got to be Steve McQueen.

My brother would always be James Garner—a totally respectable second choice.

And that left my little sister.

Inevitably, despite her protests, she always had to be the "other" American.

I will bet dollars to donuts you probably don't even remember this character. As kids, we didn't even know his name, so we made up a suitably boring name for him and called him Mickey Brown

That was who my little sister always had to be. She never got to be Steve McQueen or James Garner. In all honesty, I don't think we ever let her escape the prison; she always got shot or something in the attempt.

Needless to say, she'll never ever let my brother and I forget that.

Now, the three of us think that's a pretty good story. We laugh about it all the time. Sadly, however, I'm unable to report any personal growth involved, as this pattern repeated pretty much as long as our *Great Escape* craze lasted.

So there you have it: a story with no character arc.

What goes in real life goes for fiction as well. If you have a story in which stuff happens and it's *interesting*—but there's no character arc—that doesn't mean you might not still have a rip-roaringly grand tale on your hands.

CHARACTER ARC = STORY, NO CHARACTER ARC = SITUATION

In his *Writer* article "A big-city cop moves to a small coastal town…"

(September 2013), Jeff Lyons differentiates a *story* from a *situation*, using the following four criteria:

> [1] A situation is a problem or predicament with an obvious and direct solution. [2] A situation does not reveal character; it tests problem-solving skills. [3] A situation has no (or few) subplots, twists or complications. [4] A situation begins and ends in the same emotional space that it started in.

Number Two is especially important. A book with no character arc will still be about a protagonist who wants something, has a plan to gain that thing, and meets up with opposition that gets in his way. He'll no doubt learn a few facts and perhaps skills along the way. But he won't have to undergo a fundamental personal change in order to defeat his antagonist. Whatever Lie may be present in his life won't be challenged by the events of this story.

By Lyons's definition, Steven Spielberg's *Raiders of the Lost Ark* is a situation, not a story. Indiana Jones has no character arc. He's the same guy at the end of the movie as he was at the beginning. Did that harm the story? Not at all. Nobody (including Spielberg, who was convinced while he was making it that it was a B film) would accuse it of deep thematic grist. But it's a timeless and innovative romp that continues to charm audiences.

How to Tell the Difference Between No Arc and a Flat Arc

Flat Arcs also involve no personal inner change for the protagonist. So how is that different from a story with no arc?

The key is that Flat Arc stories still incorporate a Lie/Truth. But unlike in Change Arcs, the protagonist already possesses the Truth and is able to use it to change the characters and world *around* him. By contrast, in stories with *no* arc, there will be no battle between a Truth and a Lie.

Arc-less stories tend to show up predominately in the action/adventure genres, where the emphasis is on the physical journey/survival of the characters. At first glance, we might want to lump the whole action milieu into this mix. However, many stories of this ilk do incorporate comparatively shallow Lies and Truths, making them Flat-Arc stories.

For example, *Jurassic Park* (to return to one of my favorite examples) is essentially as much of a situation as is *Indiana Jones*, even though it incorporates a Positive Change Arc in a subplot. But unlike *Indiana Jones*, *Jurassic Park* presents its scientist protagonists as Flat-Arc characters trying to use the Truth that "*life won't be contained*" to protect and change the dangerous world in which they find themselves.

This type of Truth isn't going to be as thematically deep as Hamlet's existential "*to be or not to be*" variety, but it can still bring an added dimension even to stories that, on the surface, don't seem to require any type of arc.

Should You Write a Story With No Character Arc?

Now we come to the big question. Should you ever consider writing a story with no character arc?

There's no black or white answer to this. You *can* write a story without a character arc, and, what's more, you can write a fabulously entertaining story. If you have a story that works well based on its situation alone and you don't *want* to mess with an arc, go for it.

However, I've yet to meet the story that couldn't be improved by a thoughtful character arc, even if it's as slight as the Flat Arc in *Jurassic Park*. As Lyons says in his article:

> Situations entertain us; stories entertain *and* teach us what it means to be human.

Weigh your options. What are the pros and cons of excluding an arc from your current story? Listen to your gut—and never include a character arc just because you feel you have to.

"To exist is to change,
to change is to mature,
to mature is to go on
creating oneself endlessly."
—Henri Bergson

27

How Do I Write a Character Arc in a Series?

THESE DAYS, MORE stories than not are told as part of multi-book series—everything from trilogies to thirty-plus installments with no intended end in sight. Up to now, I've been addressing character arcs primarily within the structure of a single story, using the important structural moments in a classic Three-Act plot to anchor the timing. But what if your character's arc spans more than just three acts and one book?

2 Ways to Include Arcs in a Series

You can approach character arcs in a series in either of the two following ways:

1. One Character Arc for the Entire Series

If your series is telling one seamless, overarching story—as in, say, the Star Wars trilogy, Brent Weeks's Night Angel trilogy, Stephen Lawhead's King Raven trilogy, or Susanne Collins's Hunger Games trilogy—then you will also probably want to choose to implement one overarching character arc throughout the series. The character arc that begins in Book 1 won't be completed until the end of Book 3 (or whatever).

2. Multiple Character Arcs Throughout the Series

If each installment in your series is a complete and distinct episode—as in the Marvel movies series, Patrick O'Brian's Aubrey/Maturin series, and Ruth Downie's Roman Empire series—then you may choose to implement a new character arc for each book. In this approach, the character will encounter a new Lie in each book, which must be overcome by the end of the episode. The Lie will either be completely new and separate from previous adventures, or it will build upon the character's previous experiences. (For example, in his first movie, Thor undergoes a Positive Change Arc, which then sets up the Truth on which his Flat Arc in the second movie is based.) This approach is pretty intuitive, since it basically uses the same formula as any standalone book with a standalone character arc.

How to Structure Character Arcs in an Overarching Series

If you're writing an overarching series, you'll start by approaching your character's arc just as you would if you were writing a standalone book. All of the important structural moments (which we've discussed in previous parts) will need to be in place over the course of the story. The only difference is that the timing is spread out significantly.

Overarching Character Arcs in a Trilogy

Trilogies are comparatively easy to adapt to overarching character arcs, since their three-book format closely mirrors the three acts in a standalone book (with the First Act being the character's time of comparatively unrewarding enslavement to his Lie, the Second being his time of discovering the Truth and growing away from the Lie, and the Third being his claiming of his new empowerment via the Truth). The original Star Wars trilogy is an especially great and obvious example of how this works.

However, keep in mind that in a standalone book, the Second Act is twice as long as either the First or Third Acts. This *does not* mean the second book in your trilogy has to be twice as long as the other two. But it does mean the three acts of the overarching story won't neatly divide into one act per book. The second act will begin three-quarters of the way through the first book and end a quarter of the way through the third. Even still, adjusting the timing of the character's development (and the overall structure in general) is comparatively easy to figure out in a trilogy.

Overarching Character Arcs in a Series of Four Books (or More)

If you're writing a series of fixed length that spans *more* than three books, the same basic principles apply, but you'll have to think a little harder about adjusting the timing in order to get the arc to play out smoothly over the course of the entire series.

A four-book series is actually just as easy as a trilogy, since the Three-Act structure divides neatly into four sections (First Act, First Half of the Second Act, Second Half of the Second Act, Third Act). But the more books you add after that, the more complicated the timing and pacing gets.

Bonus Tip: Use Series to Add Even More Depth to Your Character Arcs

So far, this is all pretty straightforward, right? Either you stretch your character arc over all the books in your series, or you make a new arc for each book. But what if (shazam!) you could do *both*?

Even in an overarching series, every book needs to be complete unto itself: three acts, beginning, middle, end, opening dramatic question, ending with a resolution answering that question. Even though the main plot—and the main character arc—stretches beyond each individual book, you still have the opportunity to develop isolated aspects unique to each book.

How does that work for character arcs?

Let's say you've got an overarching character arc for your trilogy, based on a big Lie your character believes about being a coward. He's going to be working on that Lie throughout the trilogy and slowly embracing the Truth that *bravery is a choice, not an inborn virtue.*

By itself, that's probably enough to successfully float your series. But why not amp it up? Why not add layers and depth?

Each book in your series can be more than just a building block in the structure of the overarching arc. They can also be smaller, supporting, standalone arcs of their own. Each book can create a smaller arc, based on a smaller Lie—one that will ultimately contribute to your character's ability to overcome the big, overarching Lie. For example, Book 1 might feature a "mini" Lie about how *doing brave acts (e.g., stopping a mugging) is a task that belongs only to socially designated heroes* (e.g., the cops), while Book 2's Lie might be that *fear is tantamount to cowardice.*

Book 3 might feature a Lie about how *we're not responsible for doing brave things if we can remain in ignorance about the need for them.* But since Book 3 will also be the culmination of the overarching Lie, you may want to focus all your energy there for a more seamless effect.

Just as character arcs can bring untold depth and resonance to your standalone stories, they will also lift your series out of mediocrity and into memorability. Whatever they demand in complicated pacing and timing, they give back tenfold in thematic strength and character development. Don't be afraid to go the extra mile by using character arcs in a series. Your readers will adore you for it.

And that brings us to the conclusion of our exploration of character arcs! I hope you've enjoyed studying this fascinating aspect of story theory and have gleaned useful tools for telling your own stories. If you're going to write a story worthy of your amazing protagonist, the first thing you have to do is write a character arc that resonates with your readers and leaves them gasping, cheering, or crying. Or all three! "How to write character arcs?" isn't just any old question for a writer. It's one of *the* questions. Master the tenets of the Positive Change, Flat, and Negative Change Arcs, and you'll be able to write any story with confidence and skill.

Note From K.M. Weiland: Thanks so much for reading! I hope you've enjoyed learning how to write powerful and effective character arcs. Did you know that reviews are what sell books? If *Creating Character Arcs* was helpful to you, would you consider rating and reviewing it? Thank you and happy writing!

Want more writing tips?

CLAIM YOUR FREE BOOK!

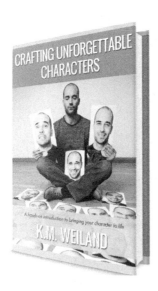

Featuring some of K.M. Weiland's most popular tips on character crafting, this book offers a firm foundation for understanding the basics of character building, as well as solid tips for troubleshooting.

Discover inspiring quotes from successful authors, writing prompts, and creativity exercises. This book gives you the tools you need to tackle your latest batch of characters.

"Exactly the information and inspiration I was looking for to liven up my characters."

kmweiland.com/free-characters-book

REFERENCES

Ackerman, Angela, Puglisi, Becca, *The Negative Trait Thesaurus* (JADD Publishing, 2013)

Bell, James Scott, *Write Your Novel From the Middle* (Compendium Press, 2014)

Bernhardt, William, *Perfecting Plot* (Babylon Books, 2013)

Gerke, Jeff, *Plot vs. Character* (Writer's Digest Books, 2010)

Hauge, Michael, *Writing Screenplays That Sell* (Collins Reference, 2011)

Lyons, Jeff, "A big-city cop moves to a small coastal town…," *The Writer*, September 2013.

McCollum, Jordan, *Character Arcs* (Durham Cress Books, 2013)

McKee, Robert, *Story* (HarperCollins, 2010)

Morris, Roz, *Writing Characters Who'll Keep Readers Captivated* (Red Season, 2014)

Phillips, Melanie Anne, Huntley, Chris, *Dramatica* (Write Brothers Press, 1999)

Schmidt, Victoria Lynn, *45 Master Characters* (Writer's Digest Books, 2011)

Sicoe, Veronica, "The 3 Types of Character Arc – Change, Growth and Fall," <http://www.veronicasicoe.com/blog/2013/04/the-3-types-of-character-arc-change-growth-and-fall/>

Vogler, Christopher, *The Writer's Journey* (Michael Wiese Productions, 2007)

Williams, Stanley D., *The Moral Premise* (Michael Wiese Productions, 2006)

ABOUT THE AUTHOR

K.M. WEILAND LIVES in make-believe worlds, talks to imaginary friends, and survives primarily on chocolate truffles and espresso. She is the award-winning and internationally-published author of the popular writing guides *Outlining Your Novel* and *Structuring Your Novel*, as well as the dieselpunk adventure *Storming*, the medieval epic *Behold the Dawn*, and the portal fantasy *Dreamlander*. When she's not making things up, she's busy mentoring other authors through her award-winning blog *Helping Writers Become Authors*. She is a native of western Nebraska. Visit her on Facebook or Twitter to participate in her Writing Question of the Day (#WQOTD). You can email her at kmweiland@kmweiland.com.

Also by K.M. Weiland

The Six Transformational Character Arcs of the Human Life

Ready to take your story's character arcs and themes to the next level? Venture far beyond the popular and pervasive Hero's Journey to explore six archetypal character arcs, representing key moments of initiation.

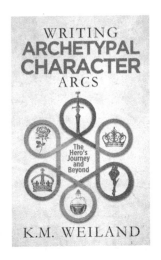

Is Structure the Hidden Foundation of All Successful Stories?

Why do some stories work and others don't? The answer is structure. In this award-winning guide, you will discover the universal underpinnings that guarantee powerful plot and character arcs.

HelpingWritersBecomeAuthors.com

Sometimes even pilots have to wing it.

*The vengeance of a monk.
The love of a countess.
The secrets of a knight.*

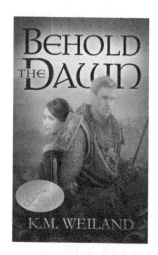

What if dreams came true?

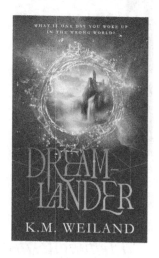

KMWeiland.com

READY TO BRAINSTORM POWERFUL ARCHETYPAL STORIES?

MAIDEN ARC

HERO ARC

QUEEN ARC

KING ARC

CRONE ARC

MAGE ARC

Use these guided meditations to dive deep into your subconscious creativity and your own instinctive understanding of archetypes.

- Listen to audio downloads of 45-61 minutes
- Explore every structural beat
- Discover your story's innate symbolism
- Buy all 6, get 1 free!